Training Library Staff and Volunteers to Provide Extraordinary Customer Service

by Julie Todaro *and* Mark L. Smith

Neal-Schuman Publishers, Inc.
New York   London

Published by Neal-Schuman Publishers, Inc.
100 William St., Suite 2004
New York, NY 10038

Printed and bound in the Unites States of America.

The paper used in this publication meets the minimum requirements of American National Standard for Information Sciences—Permanence of Paper for Printed Library Materials, ANSI Z39.48-1992.

Library of Congress Cataloging-in-Publication Data

Todaro, Julie Beth.
    Training library staff and volunteers to provide extraordinary customer service / by Julie Todaro and Mark L. Smith.
        p. cm.
    Includes bibliographical references and index.
    ISBN 1-55570-560-X (alk. paper)
    1. Library employees—In-service training. 2. Public services (Libraries) 3. Customer services. I. Smith, Mark, 1956– II. Title.
    Z668.5.T63 2006
020.71'55—dc22
                                                                    2006020705

Contents

List of Figures

Preface

Why a customer service book just for libraries? There are hundreds of books and articles describing "the importance of customer service," "how to provide good customer service," and "the significance of customers and customer service." While many of these resources offer information libraries can use, much of it is geared to for-profit environments. Libraries must adapt and often redesign conventional approaches to successfully working with users, developing and employing techniques that play to their own institutional strengths and particularities. Public, academic, school, and special libraries all assist their patrons in a way unlike any other institution or organization. Falling back on the common platitudes of commercial customer service would be insufficient at best.

Both of us have served in a variety of administrative positions at libraries of many sizes and types. Our sense of how libraries can better serve their users was developed through our practical experiences at these institutions. We hope that our hard-earned knowledge can inform and ease your own planning for staff development. Our core training philosophy—and thus the chief principle behind this book—is that it is crucially important that customer service training be a perpetual process, a fundamental part of the life of the institution. This has led us to emphasize a concept that we refer to as "continuous learning," the organization's constant reaffirmation of its commitments and ideal practices. As library directors, we know that a single well-planned and -executed training session can have tremendous effect and is often all that is possible. Whatever approach you choose to take, we firmly believe that you will find something of use in the chapters ahead.

Training Library Staff and Volunteers to Provide Extraordinary Customer Service is designed to help you accomplish the following objectives:

- Build learning into the organization's goals and strategies
- Provide a structure for assessing organizational and employee needs
- Offer supervisors, managers, and workshop leaders with "what to say" and "what to do" content they can use in both formal and on-the-run training situations
- Create a framework for gathering customer feedback
- Describe the best techniques for training staff and volunteers at all levels to respond to day-to-day interactions with customers
- Share time-effective ways of shaping instruction to match diverse staff levels
- Develop a training curriculum and process that match content to organizational and employee needs as well as learning styles
- Implement organizational processes to ensure that educational and training content are integrated into work routines and responsibilities
- Build a system for assessment and outcomes

We have strived to develop training materials you can customize to match library type, staff size, prevailing management styles, and organizational structure.

A chapter-by-chapter breakdown of the book is below.

Chapter 1, "Determining Customer Service Essentials," discusses the fundamental ground on which any customer service training must be built. It begins by going over ten crucial concerns for customer service and then proceeds to describe how customer service can be tailored for specific audiences.

Chapter 2, "Examining General Training Guidelines," explores ways to create a training program properly tailored to the needs of your staff, volunteers, and organization.

Chapter 3, "Preparing Specific Training for Library Staff and Volunteers," further delves into the particulars of customer service in the library. From finding the proper instructional strategies for each staff member to deciding when to employ those strategies, the information in this chapter is essential.

Chapter 4, "Assessing and Anticipating the Needs of Customers," helps you determine how to help your staff avert possible problems before they arise and be prepared for common situations.

Chapter 5, "Tracking and Responding to Customer Feedback," presents some of the best means to both find out how library users are feeling and communicate this information to employees.

Chapter 6, "Planning Staff-Development Days," assesses the benefits of setting time aside to improve customer service and argues for some of the most beneficial ways of doing so.

Chapter 7, "Instituting Continuous Learning in Libraries," explores the reasons why training should be made a perpetual process rather than a one-time event.

Chapter 8, "Integrating Continuous Learning with Customer Service," covers the techniques and strategies that will perpetually reaffirm a library staff's commitment to assisting the public.

Further supplementing the materials in these chapters are seven additional resources designed to function as practical tools for managers and trainers. Resource A suggests additional ways to develop policy and curriculum. Resource B provides four handouts covering reasonable standards for adult behavior. Resources C and D offer charts that will help you methodically evaluate the customer service environment. Resources E, F, and G furnish a variety of systematic means of collecting information from library users about their experiences and needs. Finally, Resource H provides a listing of Works Consulted.

We designed *Training Library Staff and Volunteers to Provide Extraordinary Customer Service* to be both an exploration of the content and methods of customer service training and a guide to introducing a new customer service approach to employees in your library. We hope that you will find it a useful and instructive tool as you go about transforming your work environment.

1

Determining Customer Service Essentials

Customer service is one of the most important content areas for training and development in today's workplace. Whether library environments are slow or busy, digital or virtual, customers have high expectations for services and resources. And while librarians may not always think of key library services as "customer" services, most, if not all, of our services—such as reference, instruction, circulation, research, and programming—are part of an overall concept of customer service. To design staff development and training for extraordinary customer service for staff, managers must be familiar with customer service issues overall, library customer service, the library's customers, and customer needs. In addition, managers must take special care to design staff development and training for extraordinary customer service for volunteers, who, if present in the library, may interact with customers in a wide variety of different and important ways.

Although there are many commercial products designed to assist with customer service training, almost all packages identify a core of issues critical to all quality customer service programs. While these core issues are articulated in a variety of ways, ten common elements can be isolated for every program. Each of these elements can and should be considered as you develop your own customer service training content. These elements should be prioritized according to your organization's needs.

Exploring Ten Crucial Concerns

Ten crucial factors underlie a library's ability to provide great customer service.

1. *Environment.* Ideally, a library should design a floor plan, create appropriate physical spaces, and purchase furniture to provide the perfect setting for meeting the needs of both general and target customers. The reality, however, is

that many, if not most, library environments have little if any control over the physical setting they can offer customers. In assessing their environment, librarians must consider all environmental elements.

- Is the furniture the appropriate size for customers? Is it "hot," or wired as necessary?
- Is the furniture positioned appropriately to protect staff, volunteers, and customers from safety hazards including networks of wires or exposed or uncovered plugs?
- Do the styles of the library environment coordinate with the community? Do they complement the neighborhood?
- Are the furniture and fixtures chosen to handle volume and type of customer use?
- Do the furniture and fixtures provide comfort, individual work space, and small-group work opportunities?
- Are the colors appropriate for a variety of activities, including individual work and study, group programs, quiet study, and small-group work?
- Do the pictures or art reflect the colors and style of the library environment or of the community or neighborhood?
- Has noise control been considered a factor in furniture choice and in building and interior design?
- Is the lighting acceptable for daytime and evening? In foyers and in primary work and reading areas of the library? Does lighting make it possible to view workstation monitors? Is the lighting appropriate for individual work, for small groups, and for large groups?
- How does the library signage contribute to customer service? What is the signage placement, color, and wording? Is the language used in signage appropriate to the community or neighborhood? Are the images in the signage used appropriately? If you cannot change signage in a facility based on cost or owing to an architect's agreements, can you add signage to attract customers or to make them feel more comfortable?

2. *Ergonomics.* Most individuals using public spaces for services and resources want a predictable little-changing or non-changing environment. Once customers, users, or students "learn an area" and how to read signs regarding how they should react to and behave within an area, it is best to maintain consistency in furniture arrangement. Place as few constraints as possible on the movement of customers throughout the library. Do not put furniture in the way of customers moving among library spaces. Are customers with special needs, such as the visually impaired, or recognized cultural (and other) differences distanced from the staff by furniture placement or size or other barriers? (See next chapter regarding unique needs.)

3. *Time.* Staff members must be aware of how their customers use their time at libraries, how they manage their time and the possible time constrictions on them. People in college environments typically have less control over their own

time and are often not aware of time issues and constraints on staff or issues relating to what they need. Public library customer timelines are often driven by the individual customer's needs and community needs as well as by other community organization timelines; therefore, staff should always plan with more than just the customer in mind and should gather data from:

- Organizational timelines
- School calendar and customers' schedules
- School assignment schedules and timelines
- Business and profit schedules
- Community, area, and neighborhood events timelines

Other issues include any ethnic or cultural time issues as well as the simplest issues of transportation and traffic patterns, such as when the bus stops or unprotected left turns, and safety issues, such as the best time to cross the street to get to the library.

4. *Customer profiles.* To provide good service, staff must gather data and prepare profiles of customers and potential customers.

- Do you know how to determine customers' learning styles or what those styles are? Do you know how they influence how you work with them and how to provide unique or customized services?
- Do your customers learn best by providing examples or instructions?
- Would audio-visual or picture or print material work better to convey information to your customers?
- What is the attention span of your customers? Is their attention span longer with some formats than with others?
- Are there cultural differences for teaching and learning that you need to honor?
- Do you have customers whose religious holidays are not widely celebrated in your organization? How should you match holiday recognitions to your community, neighborhood, or organization?
- What are the reading levels of your customers?
- Are there any special customer needs based on differently abled customers or on gender, age, interests, or reading or learning levels or styles?

5. *The human condition.* Although the phrase *human condition* is vague and can mean a variety of things depending on the situation, it still merits discussion and real consideration by those providing customer service in public environments. Librarians must gather data on what events or situations create emotions that are likely to affect their customers. Specific situations include holidays, media events or news reports, annual occurrences such as tax time, and school schedule issues such as finals and midterms. Consider the human condition situation of the college student who finds that library fines are keeping him or her from registering for classes? Deadlines, fines or "charges," and "personal forces" such as age and health contribute to what we call the human condition. Certain

situations, such as providing information of a personal or confidential nature, helping a student to finish a difficult assignment, or handling fines, will require special customer service care.

6. *Body language and proxemics.* Educate staff and volunteers in how their body language, when dealing with customers, can convey messages. Whether a staff member actually feels the way that the body language communicates is not the issue. The issue is how customers perceive the attitude and comfort level of the person assisting them. Consider these nonverbal cues:

- Arms akimbo usually means an unhappy person.
- Arms crossed over the chest indicates a "Don't talk to me" message, or "I feel uncomfortable in this situation," or (even worse) "You [the customer] make me feel uncomfortable."

What messages are staff members and volunteers sending when customers approach them while they staff public service desks?

- Do employees at reference or circulation desks have their heads buried in special projects for long periods of time?
- Are employees at public service desks talking on a telephone without signaling they will be finished soon?
- Do staff members interrupt one customer's discussion with them to answer another customer's question?

Good customer service also means that employees must learn to handle large numbers of customers waiting for assistance. Also, employees must learn to juggle persons who are waiting for assistance in person with those who are calling in or are on hold. Yet most staff and volunteers must also work on other tasks while at public service desks. Customers need to know that interrupting staff at some times is okay. It is not enough simply to lift your head from a project if you fail to put down your pencil, remove your elbows from the desk, or in some other way signal a closure with one task and a willingness to assume another.

Proxemics, a study of spatial relationships, examines space and comfort. Although several of these areas have been addressed under other content areas, the issues bear repeating, and there are several aspects of this research that apply to libraries.

- How is territory defined in your area? Are all customers comfortable, or do some feel there is no space for them near the staff member assisting them?
- Are your customers, because of the library's physical arrangement or lack of space, shuttled from one place to another?
- Are you aware of how far from or close to customers you stand?
- Do you touch customers, such as hugging someone or patting someone's arm? Could there be misinterpretations? It should not be assumed that anyone, regardless of age, likes to be touched or hugged.

7. *Staff and volunteer parameters.* To empower employees, managers must define just what the parameters of employee "power" are. The first step is to

determine what employees can or cannot offer customers when assisting them. Staff need guidance in handling requests that go beyond services or that ask staff to shortcut steps in procedures or break policy.

- How do you determine what staff think and practice regarding parameters? An interesting exercise is to present both staff members and managers with a list of customer service areas and then have each list what they can and cannot do for customers. Next, compare the two lists so that managers can see how staff members view and interpret policies and procedures.

Parameters should also be identified for volunteers serving customers in the library. This identification is especially important, since volunteers typically have different roles and thus different customer service interactions. In addition, it is not atypical to have volunteer power and staff power differ in imposing organizational policy.

- How do you determine what volunteers think and practice regarding parameters? As described in assessing staff member parameters, an interesting exercise is to present volunteers with a list of customer service areas and then have each list what they can and cannot do for customers. Next, compare the two lists so that managers can see how volunteers differ from themselves, as well as how volunteers differ from staff members, in their view and interpretation of policies and procedures.

8. *Customer feedback.* While in-depth customer evaluation is always good, there are several ways to get immediate customer feedback from sometimes typically silent customers. Besides the classic evaluation cards given to, for example, restaurant customers, there are many ways to get immediate or quick feedback.

- Make a "How am I doing?" three-by-five-inch card or bookmark with four to six questions such as: Did you find what you needed? Did I answer your questions? Did that material give you the information you wanted? Public service staff can put these in prominent locations as well as in materials at the check-out desk, making sure to post answers with questions. Staff should also ask customers these questions at workstations and be prepared to offer additional help or direct customers to someone who can help them.
- Signs requesting general or specific comments might be posted on white butcher paper (non-bleeding!) or poster board so that customers can write comments or answers directly on the paper.

Your training program should also instruct staff and volunteers in how to respond to customer feedback and questions.

9. *Positive communication.* Part of any complete customer service program is the design and adoption of a policy of positive communication that focuses on recommended word or phrase choices, intonation, inflection, and volume to match recommended body language and proxemics. Staff must find a speaking voice that is positive and respectful of customers, including younger people, and avoid demeaning or negative language.

The following are examples of positive language phrases and sentences that can be used in any customer service interaction. Providing phrases rather than complete scripts will allow staff a greater level of flexibility and will give them a valuable tool to maintain control over a variety of encounters. Staff and volunteers will also benefit by having an array of phrases that represent the kind of negative language to avoid.

Figures 1.1 and 1.2 offer optimal phrases and behaviors that employees can use and language that they should seek to avoid in customer service environments.

Figure 1.1
Ideal Communications Strategies

- "We have several choices in this situation..."
- "What I can do is... What I can't do is..."
- "Rather than doing it this way, you need to do it this way..."
- "I hear what you are saying..."
- "Would it be possible for you to..."
- "Would you please..."
- "I appreciate your point; however..."
- "I can understand how you would feel this way..."
- "You have a point..."
- "You're right... however..." (this practice is known as selective agreement)
- "I would be happy to listen to you..."
- "Let me think now..."
- "Please don't yell..."
- "I need more explanation on..."
- "Could you repeat that a little more slowly?"
- Actively listen by interjecting or saying, "You're right; that is a problem"; "I can see how you would be upset by that"; or "That would concern me, too."
- "I can see that I am not helping you or giving you the information that you need. Let me have _____ call you back... or let me have _____ speak with you..."
- Describe your feelings at that moment: "I am confused by your statement." "I am concerned at your statement."
- "What would you like me to do?"
- "As I understand it, you want..."
- "I'm willing to... if you're willing to..."
- Repeat what they have said to you, slowly, stating it as they have.
- Restate what they say, but don't continue to restate and restate hoping to find a way they will understand. Often repeating something several times, both your words and their words, will make the point.
- Maintain control of the situation by your consistency, tone of voice, eye contact, and posture.
- Admit that you were wrong or that the organization makes mistakes sometimes and, if appropriate, in this instance— but admit to only what was really wrong—"Yes, we were in error in this instance; however, in the case of the mail on your end..." Avoid beginning with their "wrong," such as "You did this..."
- "Excuse me, but I don't feel that I have to listen to that kind of language... I would be happy to speak with you at another time when we can avoid this language..." or...
- "I don't feel comfortable discussing this issue with this language... Let's talk another time when I feel we are both calmer..."

(cont'd.)

Figure 1.1
Ideal Communications Strategies (Continued)

- Let a three-second moment of silence take place after someone has spoken so that he or she has to say something else other than the comments. If someone asks if you are there, reply, "Yes, I'm listening and taking notes to better answer you."
- You might hear statements or phrases such as "I didn't get the document you were supposed to send me," or "I can't believe you or your office is so inefficient." Ignore the second phrase or the direct attack against you or your group or team as if the individual didn't say it and handle the first statement. You can even let the person know you are doing this by saying, "Rather than talking about this, let's address your specific need here..."
- To let others know you care or are concerned, but have limited time or you want to create additional time to handle a situation, identify up front how much time you have to work with someone. For example, "Tell me what you need today; I have about five minutes prior to a meeting or appointment, but I can help you later..."
- Use the phrases "What it sounds like you're saying is..."; "Maybe I misunderstood...let me see if I have this straight..."; "Here's what I understood you to say..."
- If someone angrily begins an interchange with you, greet the individual as if he or she isn't angry.

Figure 1.2
Behaviors and Phrases to Avoid

- Do not feel that you must respond (such as "uh huh") during an especially bad interchange. Use the three-beat silence.
- Do not say, "No one has ever had this problem before..."
- Do not constantly restate. Customers concentrate on the variety of ways and think that you are being evasive.
- Avoid always having to have the last word. That is considered an aggressive act.
- Do not interrupt a diatribe.
- Do not finish people's sentences.
- After an especially bad encounter, even if you know that the person has finished, wait the three beats; use the "taking notes comment."
- Avoid using words that escalate anger—negatives, "you," "you're." Avoid phrases that escalate anger—"Why didn't you..."; "Don't you know that..."; "Don't you ever..."; "This always happens..."
- Do not say, "That's not my job," or "I can't do that," or "I can't help you" and use frustrating generalities. Be specific and say, "I don't have the answer to that, but I know that _____ does. Either you can ask them or I can ask them. What would you prefer?"
- Do not say, "I can't do anything..." You can say, "I can't do anything more," or "I'm sorry, I can only listen in this case and recommend..."
- You do not have to tolerate profanity or name calling. Staff and volunteers should know that they can state that up front as soon as it starts.

---

10. *Practice, practice, practice.* We can learn to provide excellent customer service through a variety of methods of teaching and learning in the workplace. The following techniques ensure that training is incorporated into the daily work of the organization and that your continuous-learning program will continue throughout the year:

- Analysis, self-assessment and observation. Conduct self-assessments and employee observation. Following training, employees can identify levels of progress through completing self-assessment checklists that indicate comfort levels with competencies and competency achievement. Employers can use observation worksheets to assess customer service interactions. Employees can team for small-group or peer-to-peer teaching and support.

- Example or role-model observation of others. Exceptional customer service interactions by staff with advanced customer service skills can be identified throughout the organization and used as points of reference for employees seeking specific opportunities for observing how to deal with an organization's customers.
- Study and teaching with scenarios, cases, and simulations. Many libraries use "stories," or scenarios, to illustrate the application of content to similar work settings or similar customers. These stories, cases, or simulations provide staff with frames of reference for customer service content. (We will discuss scenarios and scripting at greater length in later chapters.)
- Guidelines and actual wording. Although the goal of training and development is to offer staff and volunteers the content and competency development to be able to act independently and comfortably with all types of customers in all types of situations, often the frequently reoccurring, most difficult, or conflict-ridden situations need specific wording to maintain consistency in handling.
- Practice, practice, practice. The best teaching and learning takes place in learning settings and then is reinforced in extensive and, often, very structured practice sessions following training and development sessions. Applying content learned in customer service workshops is a critical step in a successful program, and managers need to design the post-training structures for ongoing teaching and learning opportunities.

Providing Help to Children and Youth

When researching customer service and children and youth, one finds few references to serving children as customers but many to attracting children as customers. Most commercial packages for customer service training do not specifically address customer service issues or programs of service for children and young people. The ten common elements identified as core elements for programs as outlined above, can also be used as a foundation for training staff and volunteers to assist children and youth, but there are specific elements under each of the ten categories unique to serving this target population.

1. *Environment.* Although the majority of public libraries have children's spaces, many do not provide—owing to space or other constraints—a space for preteens or teens and young adults. Libraries should make every attempt to define spaces that meet the needs of all age levels of young people. These considerations should include pictures and artwork, appropriate furniture (size, portability, flexibility, colors, and comfort), and combinations of quiet space for individuals

and space for active learning for small groups. Some of the best spaces result from having teen panels or advisory groups assist in ensuring the contemporary nature of artwork and both the choice of colors and style of décor. While it is important for all customers to feel comfortable, it is most critical for young people to feel as if there is space defined specifically to meet their needs.

2. *Ergonomics.* While most individuals using public spaces for services and resources want a predictable little- or non-changing environment, children, pre-teens, and teenagers often prefer an environment that is updated frequently. Although it is important for this target population to find its resources, flow is less important and takes a backseat to an environment that is fun, is welcoming, and peaks customers' curiosity and promotes discovery.

3. *Time.* Children have less control over their time and often use the library based on their larger school schedule, usually after school and weekend schedule needs are met. It is critical for staff to identify those time "drivers" for children and young people, including assessing family situations to see if children and young people will be coming with families, coming alone, or using a variety of means of transportation to use the library. In public libraries, staff need to know organizational timelines, the school calendar, after-school activities, school assignment schedules and timelines, and community and neighborhood events and timelines. In school libraries, librarians must schedule around school schedules and activities. The presence or lack of flexible scheduling and the overall integration of the library into the curriculum and information literacy program in the school must also be taken into account. In academic settings there may be a variety of programs that are designed to serve students co-enrolled in high schools and colleges, serving families of college or adult students as well as general students from the community. In spite of the fact that the physical environment may not be set up for serving these customer groups, assignment timelines, area school schedules, and the higher education schedule must integrate to offer good customer service.

4. *Customer profiles.* Although profiles of children and young people are harder data to gather, at the very least general developmental information must be gathered for children and young people and used to provide librarians with background on how best to address this target population. Developmental stages include language levels, mobility issues, emotional maturity, intellectual abilities, independent or self-directed abilities for work and play, communication skills, social development, and learning and reading levels. (See the Resource Tools for specific examples of matching quality customer service to developmental stages.)

5. *The human condition.* Considering human condition issues is just as important in serving children and young people as it is for adults. While some of the same conditions that affect adults affect the younger target populations, there are unique conditions that apply to younger customers, including communication challenges related to adolescence; how children and young people sort into small and large groups, and social and learning concerns related to youth reading (or not reading) on grade level.

6. *Body language and proxemics.* Children and young people observe the body language of adults as much as adults do. Often adults serving this target population are uncomfortable with children of certain ages, children and young people in groups rather than as individuals, and gender and age issues. The concern here, as with adults, is how customers perceive the attitude and comfort level of the adult assisting them.

Proxemics is a major issue when adults provide customer service to children and young people. There is a tendency among many adults to have automatic contact (such as hugging, grabbing or touching an arm or hand) with children. Often, these contacts are inappropriate. Touching children—such as patting them on the head and hugging them—can be misinterpreted. Management will want to train employees to understand that they must approach working with young people with as much care as they use for adults, perhaps more.

7. *Staff and volunteer parameters.* Staff and volunteer parameters for serving young people must be discussed with the same care as for adults. Sample parameters might include checking out adult materials to children and young people and assisting children in accessing Web sites.

8. *Customer feedback.* Seeking ways for children and youth to indicate comfort levels and degrees of satisfaction is an important part of the customer service program. Librarians will want to identify unusual ways to get children and young people talking about their likes, dislikes, and service needs. Current methods of involvement can include forming and using an advisory panel, establishing a blog for input on services, and building Web pages with methods of inputting ideas online.

9. *Positive communication.* The best possible communication is a critical element of a quality customer service plan for children and young people. Staff and volunteers must learn specific techniques for positive and respectful use of language for general service as well as for handling conflict.

10. *Practice, practice, practice.* In trying to practice the best possible techniques, working with advisory panels affords librarians to get "real life" practice and simulations. Other recommended methods for practice include scenarios and case method. Scenarios are typically short outlines of events, usually in sequence. Case methods are longer descriptions of a situation with broad, more in-depth content on the larger environment, and a wide variety of elements that set the tone, describe a situation, and profile employees and customers. In addition, the design (with advisory panel assistance) of both guidelines and wording for scripts to use is highly recommended.

Determining Important Elements

Librarians will have a number of unique concerns when considering the development of profiles, scripts, scenarios, and other tools to build the best possible communication with customers. These unique elements dictate care with language, special assistance, and unique signage, to name just a few, and include the following:

- *Political correctness.* Since September 11, 2001, librarians have found themselves considering how society regards foreign-born population or individuals who look like they are part of a group that may be at the center of a political issue. Sensitivity should also be exercised with groups such as older customers or persons with disabilities or special needs.
- *Language.* Consider not only positive phrases but also the right language to make customers feel welcome.
- *Signage.* Signage is an important consideration for all customers, and it is of special concern for the non-English speaker. Can non-English speakers understand words or phrases used in signs? Can these customers understand the images used in signage?
- *New adult English speakers and non-English speakers.* These customers will have special needs and expectations that require an approach to customer service that respects their heritage and cultural differences.
- *Technology.* How will your staff work with customers who are not as technologically astute as others?

In addition to these, your staff will encounter a wide variety of customer interactions, including in-person, virtual, digital, and synchronous (real) and asynchronous time.

Establishing an Exceptional Environment

Much of the challenge of effective customer service training is getting your staff to see the library from the customer's point of view. When staff work in the same place every day, they tend not to notice their environment. Signs that have been up for months or years become invisible, and signs that are needed are not considered because everyone knows where things are. Ergonomically disastrous furniture arrangements are not noticed because the staff seldom sit at the public reader chairs and tables. Interior design elements such as pictures on the wall, worn carpet, and poor lighting are merely familiar elements that are no longer noticed. Customers notice these elements either consciously or subconsciously, and the environment will exert significant influence over the customer's library experience.

Signage

While signage may not be the first thing that leaps to your mind when you think of quality customer service, good signage can

- Give customers the basic information they need to be self-starters
- Provide a backup for staffing during general or low staffing periods
- Reduce staff interactions for directional customer assistance, thus freeing them up for more in-depth assistance. Consider signage that empowers customers to assist themselves and their families rather than be dependent on staff.

General categories for signage include:

- *Directional signage* for external customer needs (bathrooms, water fountains, elevators, exits, and so forth)
- *Mounted signs* indicating major functional areas to indicate use or function of a specific area
- *Floor designations* for directing customers to frequently sought after locations (including carpeting, flooring surfaces, and arrows on the floor showing customers the way to the meeting room)
- *Hardware signs* for user information, such as services provided, user identification, sign-up
- *Hardware signs* with instructions for use such as how to boot up, how to view microfiche or computer files, how to copy in color or to enlarge, where to position the paper to copy or scan properly, and how to send jobs to the printer
- *"Bigger picture" environmental signage*, such as a guide to the service area or a floor map or guide
- *Web-based "signage"* such as maps and tours as well as Web information that duplicates or provides content for using the library
- *Coordinated signs* as to color, lettering, signatures, images used, and language, as well as concern for temporary signs ("meetings today"), permanent signs ("no cell phone use"), and signs "in waiting" ("printers down today")
- *Employee or functional area business cards* (standard business cards for the staff on duty, a pocket-sized reference card that indicates hours of availability, who to call, and so forth)

Staff will need training to see signs from the customer point of view and to learn how not to become frustrated when customers ask questions that staff thought were answered with a sign. In general, staff should be trained to look out for customers that appear to be puzzled and not assume that signs will answer all their questions.

One specific area of concern has to do with self-check machines. Many libraries, especially public and academic libraries, have found that self-check machines can be successful devices for freeing staff from routine interactions. This savings in staff time, theoretically, is redirected to allow staff to provide more support to customers in other areas that require more individualized attention, such as reference or readers' advisory service. In actuality, however, many members of the public are often confused about this new technology and encounter difficulties in using the machines. The best scenario in many libraries is to train staff to be attuned to customers who need assistance, to guide them to the machines and walk them through the charge of materials. This practice can also be used to achieve wonderful customer service involving other machines, such as the copier, the microfiche/film reader-printer, Internet-usage scheduling terminals, and public PCs (personal computers).

Additional signage issues should be considered when dealing with volunteers who may be involved in customer service activities. Concerns surrounding volunteers and signage include whether volunteers are clear on what library signage means both from a customer's point of view and from a library worker's point of view and whether volunteers can interpret signage for customers they may be assigned to assist.

Ergonomics

Ergonomics, the science of work, is a field of study devoted to designing work spaces around worker needs and job tasks, client needs, and the organization's services. When work spaces and public spaces are designed ergonomically, there are fewer risks of injury and illness, there is greater productivity, there is a better quality of work life, and there is improved customer service resulting from the above. Issues in ergonomics include the desire for a suitable work environment for staff and customers with concerns for climate, lighting, noise, and related hardware issues; workstations, furniture, and hardware issues such as display panels; and equipment such as copiers, scanners, fiche and film machines, and circulation system components.

Additional work space issues include placement of furniture and other library elements such as shelving and placement of hardware based on cables and wiring.

Interior Design

The stereotypical library of yesteryear is certainly not the norm of today's library and information environment. Public, academic, school, and special library environments range from the most contemporary architecture to new classical, as well as a blend of the two. Whether the library is completely new; an old, renovated location; or both, interior design elements for public spaces are complicated owing to the need for balancing print and technology, the need for flexibility (for individual, small-group, and large-group usage, and the need for space for workers and customers that meets the widest variety of seemingly ever-changing needs). Interior design elements encompass aspects of ergonomics as well as specific concerns for libraries such as signage. Design elements to be considered include:

- Color
- Floor plans of basic design of library (including walls and windows)
- Furniture
- Spatial arrangement of furniture
- Texture
- Lighting
- Plants
- Art (paintings, prints, murals, and so forth)
- Lighting and fixtures
- Acoustics as it relates to types of and arrangement of furniture, room dividers, and so forth
- Signage (interior and exterior)
- Window and wall treatments

2

Examining General Training Guidelines

Since you are reading this book, it is probably safe to assume that you already have some ideas about what aspects of customer service training your library organization's staff volunteers (or both) most need. You might be a library director or department manager who thinks that your staff is doing pretty well with some facets of public service, but not others. Perhaps you feel that some staff members or volunteers "get it" and others do not. Maybe you are approaching a large new project, such as a building move or renovation, the introduction of a new service, a new automation system, or other major change, and you want to be sure that your staff introduce this change to the public in appropriate and positive ways. You may even be a technical services or behind-the-scene employee who has now been assigned to a public service desk, or you may manage "techie" staff who are experts in technical areas but do not excel at public service interactions with peers and public service staff.

In fact, your reaction to this chapter might be to skip it altogether, saying to yourself, "I know exactly what I want the staff to know; I just need help in how to teach them." That might be true, but before your ideas about what you think you want to teach them get completely set in concrete, we recommend that you take time to test your assumptions. The benefits of the exercises in this chapter are fourfold:

1. To be sure that your ideas and approaches will be accepted and supported by both your staff and your superiors
2. To assess commercial packages or benchmark packages from other institutions to integrate them into your content
3. To design a curriculum that most directly addresses the needs of your staff and clientele
4. To make the most effective use of the training resources and opportunities available to you

This last point may be the most critical. Even if you were to have unlimited resources available to you to conduct training, you will have only limited opportunities to interact with staff and volunteers to deliver that training. To be effective, training content must be focused and targeted. To be focused, it must be thoughtfully developed. This chapter will begin by guiding you through the thought process necessary to develop focused, targeted, and thoughtful training. We will then offer a framework for specific content that can be useful in any library organization.

Clarifying Management Expectations

There are moments in the lives of organizations when the leaders must lead. Even in the most horizontally oriented organizations, the time will come when managers must act to assess the needs of the organization and set a decisive course for improvement. If, as they should, managers have their positions by virtue of their experience, education, and proven ability to lead, then they must be able to take a global, or big-picture, view of their organization to determine what would improve the quality of service provided under the sphere of their authority. They must be able to assess the situation in their library or library department and evaluate the performance of their staff against what they as managers expect of them. Also, what is taught is integrally related to the vision, mission, and culture of the organization.

For these reasons, establishing expectations for what excellent customer service in a library or library department should look like is a uniquely management function. To arrive at these expectations, however, one should not toss them off the top of one's head or scribble them on a cocktail napkin. To be effective and far-reaching, these expectations will take some time, information, and thoughtful discussion among all members of the management team in order to be developed. And because every organization is at a slightly different stage in its efforts to provide excellent customer service, organizational leaders may require different types and quantities of information. In the next chapter, we will discuss more fully the differences in training approaches that are imposed by size and type of library, but that discussion will begin here with some consideration of how the nature of your organization will influence priorities for training content.

As you consider your customer service training program, you should start with a scan of your organization to determine just exactly where you are starting from and what obstacles you may confront.

Committing to Excellent Customer Service

What is the level of commitment in your library to excellent customer service? Are you the only one talking about this? Is there a lot of talk but no action, or are you at a point where some training is being provided but management generally accepts that it needs to do more? Is it possible that your organization has a full-blown program for customer training with a carefully developed curriculum and full exploitation of all training opportunities? For the sake of this discussion, we should rule out this last scenario, since if that were the case, you would have little need to turn to a book of this sort.

If your library is like most organizations, you are neither starting from absolute scratch nor do you have a full-blown, highly integrated training program. More than likely, you or one or more of your employees have attended a customer service workshop and have returned with a recognition that the library needs to establish an education and training program to build customer service skills. Managers—based on employee recommendations—may well have signed on to the need to train staff in some aspects of technical or customer service skills, but the organization is not yet fully actualizing all of the opportunities, including available workshop content. For larger libraries—especially those with multiple departments and locations—or libraries with a larger project on the near horizon, this may be a particularly acute challenge.

Wherever you are in the process of movement toward development of a customer service training program, you must begin by discussing the situation with your colleagues. Unless you are in a very small library with a small number of staff and/or volunteers, you cannot implement a comprehensive customer service program alone. You must raise the question of what your employees need to know in a management team meeting or with your supervisor. And even if you are in a small library, you should discuss your ideas with your parent organization, library board, city manager, principal, or academic manager or with other key players. Before you introduce the topic, think through what you believe excellent customer service should look like in your library. Be methodical, gradual, and strategic. Assess the presence or lack of customer service focus in organizational documents and in umbrella organizational documents. Offer to take a lead role in efforts to gather customer satisfaction data with existing customer service practices and interactions. Focus on the most serious issues identified first. Get your ideas and data results on this topic into every meeting until a training program becomes an organizational priority. Let your enthusiasm for this idea be the spark that starts the process in your library.

Connecting Customer Service to the Library's Mission

As you begin to consider what you want your staff and/or volunteers to know in relation to your library organization, keep in mind the mission or vision statements of your organization and any customer service values you may have identified in your scan of the environment. Put your customer service efforts in the context of any planning documents that your library may already have adopted. For example, if your public library has engaged in a "Planning for Results" process, relate your goals for customer service to whatever Service Roles your library has adopted. If your academic or school library exists within the context of any campus-wide goal-setting processes, these should be taken into account. Campus or school district plans should be assessed for any customer service goals or values. By doing so, your plan for customer service training will be seen as feeding the goals of the parent organization and, thus, may be more readily adopted by individuals and governing boards up the organization chain of command. And do not discount the possibility that they may even have funding to support your training effort.

Moving from Expectation to Practice

Once you have successfully launched the discussion of management expectations, the next question concerns itself with where you are now in relation to those expectations. This is another way of asking, "How much will it take to change our behaviors?" This discussion will require that you refine your targets for your staff's customer service performance. You can probably expect for this to be a lively conversation; it is likely that some of your colleagues differ on how they perceive the level of customer service currently provided in your organization, as well as the need for change. Data and benchmarking will help with this discussion: output and outcome usage data, customer satisfaction surveys, suggestion box results, and anecdotal feedback will help you to define how well you are doing in meeting customers' needs. Whatever you set as the desired targets for your customer service program, remember that management expectation should parallel customer expectation. You cannot define your own standards for customer service until you have some idea of what your library customers expect.

Depending on the resources available to you, you may wish to start small or, if you are facing implementation of a new project, you may decide to focus on customer service practice around that activity. Regardless of how limited or extensive your project, be sure to document and quantify your goals and identify the outcomes. Your overall goal may be for your staff and/or volunteers to be more helpful to customers, but you should define that helpfulness in terms of some quantifiable goal or, at the very least, measurable outcomes. Examples of customer service outcomes include:

- Customers, addressing the issue of fines owed with circulation staff, indicated a "high level of satisfaction" when queried following circulation desk interactions.
- Parents, who attended at least four out of five lapsit programs, chose "excellent customer service" when completing postlapsit program surveys.
- Participating caregivers from childcare centers, who have used the library during fall ____, indicated in postvisit interviews that customer service was one of the top three services provided by the library's youth services department.
- Students returning to the library, after in-class visits from librarians, gave the library's customer service interaction a score of ____ or better on customer exit surveys.

As you begin to define your goals and outcomes, your plan for customer service training content will begin to come into focus.

Outcomes of staff and volunteer training examples include:

- Staff members, following customer service training, indicate their comfort level with solving customer service conflicts at circulation or reference are "more comfortable" or "significantly more comfortable."
- Staff members, assessing scripts created for dealing with customers about increased fines and fees, indicate that scripts "meet institutional needs" for customer interactions.
- Volunteers, in completing training in stack maintenance/referring customers "out of the stacks," indicate they are "more comfortable" or "significantly more comfortable" in their role in referring customers they encounter while performing stack maintenance. Employees who work in the stacks (shelvers, stack maintenance employees, librarians who are weeding, assessing gaps, and so forth) need specific scripts on how to assist patrons in finding what they need from the appropriate person (e.g., referring customers to reference desks or circulation desks).
- Volunteers, following the online training modules, score the Likert Scale training evaluation at the higher levels of 6 or 7, indicating higher levels of enjoyment with online training content and format. A Likert Scale is a measuring or rating scale—used in surveys developed by the social sciences researcher Rensis Likert—that measures or gauges attitudes, reactions, and levels of agreements with statements. Categories of response can include statements such as "strongly agree," "agree," "disagree," "strongly disagree," and so forth.

Defining Client Groups

While defining client groups has always been more of a challenge for public librarians than for academic, school, and special libraries, this is a question that pertains to all libraries. Regardless of the library's type, target groups can vary greatly depending on the nature of the institution's community and the range of projects in which the library is currently engaged. Your customer service priorities may in fact be driven by projects that are targeted to specific groups. Indeed, one of the points of your training effort may be to sensitize your staff to the needs of a segment of the population that has been historically misunderstood and, possibly, underserved. If this target population is defined by age, race, ethnicity, or gender, you will find yourself asking some specific questions about how the needs of these client groups differ from those of other client groups.

This is where management should be careful to test its assumptions. You may feel that you are uniquely in touch with the needs of a particular client group. Perhaps you are of the same ethnic group as your target population, or perhaps you have had prior experience in serving the client group. While your experience will provide extremely helpful information to your management group in serving the target clientele, there is no substitute for asking target group members what they would like to see in terms of library service.

If you have a client group that typically does not enter the library, the type of customer service the group's members have received may provide the key. When they visited the library, did they feel welcome? Upon visiting, or when they now visit, do they perceive that the library is theirs or that the library provides services and resources for them? Do they find it easier or more comfortable to satisfy their information needs elsewhere? Does management or the staff perceive that the target group is well served? For that matter, does the staff even know that the target population exists in the community? These are the questions that you will consider as you begin to define your client groups.

As you move toward defining your client groups, remember to consider the distinction between internal and external clients. In library work, we tend to focus on the external customer: the library customer. But library staffs often also have internal clients. Departments such as technical services, automation, public relations, administration, and human resources have both internal and external customers. While at times they may not be as visible, these staffs' customer service skills are extremely vital to the smooth operation of the organization. In addition, libraries will need to include umbrella organizational departments (counseling, the school nurse, classroom faculty, other city departments) in their focus on excellent service and decide if these customer or customer areas are external or internal.

Agreeing on Training Priorities

Having tested your assumptions by examining the foregoing considerations, you should begin to have a clearer idea of the customer service training needs in your organization. Informed by some basic data gathering and discussion with your colleagues, you should understand better the scope, function, and expected outcomes of your training effort. But before you can complete the process of establishing your customer service training priorities, you will also have to consider a series of other organizational issues that will influence the content of your training. The following environmental factors will further shape the establishment of your training priorities.

Funding

The amount of monetary support you have for your training effort will determine whether you are hiring outside consultants to come in and train your staff and volunteers, sending staff to seminars, or using in-house trainers and a locally developed curriculum. Most organizations use a combination of these means; but packaged programs are expensive, and you will want to consider whether you would rather spend the money on those resources or would rather develop your own content. Contrary to what you may hear in the commercial sector, a business or library can design, deliver, and maintain a quality customer service program at little or no out-of-pocket cost, but with (as with all training) an investment of organizational time and effort.

Trainers and Their Areas of Expertise

If you are going to train in-house, are there persons locally who are able to train your staff and volunteers? Are they experienced trainers, and have you observed them presenting? One key question in this regard is whether you will develop your curriculum and go find trainers or have your content be driven by the expertise of available trainers. As you develop your training content, you may have to consider who is available to you to provide the training. Neighboring libraries, umbrella organization or district human resources or training and development, or your regional library networks, consortia, or systems might prove to be resources for affordable and qualified trainers.

Project-oriented Training

One important aspect of your training curriculum will be whether it is driven by—instead of, or along with, a general program—the approach of a large project, new service, or other environmental change. A classic example would be the introduction of a new automation system in the library. Because this is a huge change that affects nearly all public service staff, a new automation system presents a traumatic moment for staff. Tempers will run high, patience will grow short, and the opportunity to mishandle this important change at the management-to-staff and the staff-to-public levels is great. Good managers will want the public to be unaware of the new automation system or, if they know about it at all, to believe that it is a great improvement for the library. Good managers will not want staff to articulate and blame the "stupid new automation system" for every problem that is encountered in any transaction. To keep things running smoothly, customer service training will need to be built into the other types of training that are required in shifting to a new automated system. The same would be true if the library were launching any new service, imposing new fines or fees, instituting new geographic boundaries, or altering services or resources. Handling charges as well as the introduction of new or different resources services offers great opportunities for positive public relations, but staff members need to know how to communicate this to the public and to interact with the public regarding the new services. The more attention that these services get in the press, the more critical staff-public interaction will be.

Judging Education and Experience

Developing an effective training content will depend on where your staff and volunteers are starting from, in terms of not only their current customer service skills as discussed above but also their prior training and experience. How many of your staff are in their teens or twenties? How many have college degrees or prior library or public service customer experience? How many have master's of library science (MLS) degrees? How many library workers are volunteers with no basic knowledge of libraries and therefore possibly no knowledge of library

---

Figure 2.1
Case Study: Cerritos Library

When is the time right to launch a comprehensive program in customer service? While a customer service program can begin at any time, the opening of a new library building offers an ideal opportunity to make a break with practices of the past and fashion an entirely new vision of how library staff will serve the public. A new building will also bring many new patrons into the library. Having our best customer service practices in place will help ensure that our relationship with these new patrons gets off to a good start.

One of the most spectacular recent examples of the opportunity offered by a new building can be found at the Cerritos Library. In that southern California town, City Librarian Waynn Pearson led the design and building of a spectacular "Library of the Future" that is part library and part interactive museum, complete with a *T. Rex* (*Tyrannosaurus rex*) skeleton stalking the children's room and a 15,000-gallon fish tank that greets visitors as they enter the library. But Pearson knew that the library consisted of more than just books, computers, and exhibits. He knew that for this library to become a total learning environment, the staff had to not only share but also actively embrace that vision.

Pearson explains to visitors to the Cerritos Library how he used the new building as a starting point to develop in staff a whole new way of seeing their jobs. The effort to transform staff attitudes began two years prior to moving in and continued throughout the construction phase. Pearson began by buying them hard hats and taking them to the construction site to see the progress of the building. He got them excited about the project, which, in turn, got them excited about their roles in the new building. In the new library, the staff are challenged to put their avocations to use in supporting the library. One of the library's pages, a huge movie buff, is asked to recommend film books for purchase. Such responsibilities create "buy-in" among staff at all levels because they empower staff to share in the mission of the library. Pearson sums it up with this observation: "You have to nurture the human spirit if you really want change to occur."

Jackie Stetson, the library operations supervisor, explains that during the construction phase a staff team was empowered to recommend how the library's core operations would function in the new building. To do this, team members had to meet with other employees in their sections and bring their suggestions and ideas back to the team. In this way, this team became a conduit for ideas to flow from staff to management. Everyone's ideas were considered, and those with particular passions, such as the film-buff page, were encouraged to put those interests to work for the library. It is not hard to see how these staff felt an increased sense of self-esteem, which translates to not only enthusiasm for and loyalty toward their library but also a heightened morale.

The Cerritos Library also developed its own brand of customer service, which it calls "Wow Service." All staff receive repeated and ongoing Wow Service training. Staff are trained to consider library patrons as "guests," and they are encouraged to take time to learn their names. Cerritos also stresses the importance of getting staff out from behind their desks, where they can interact with the public. The library designed desks that made it effortless to get out from behind the desk and low monitors that made it easier to see and be seen. All staff wear name badges (first names only). Some staff—called library aides, the next classification up from page—are given headsets, through which they are summoned and sent throughout the library to help serve guests and solve a variety of issues. And staff are trained to recognize "emotional leakage" (in themselves and others); that is, the universal tendency to bring one's personal problems to work. Stetson states that this concept caught on like wildfire, especially among the library's younger staff. It is not uncommon for one staff member to admonish another by saying, "You're leaking!"

As fun as the Cerritos Library is (and it is so much fun!), the enthusiasm and positive attitude of the library's staff are what make it a truly special place.

---

customer service? These factors will impact what you teach and how you teach, since learning styles tend to differ by age and background. While there is a basic level of customer service training for all staff, different levels or categories of staff may need a secondary level of training that might be considered advanced or specialized training. Examples of this include:

Pages

Beyond basic training, pages need to have skills that assist them in providing basic service "in the stacks" and the training to assist them in connecting customers who stop them in the stacks to staff who can assist them. Pages, if told only to "assist customers," may end up attempting to provide reference assistance. Typically, pages are taught to understand the reference process to the point that they are able to recognize certain customer inquiries as reference interactions. It may also happen as often these employees are not typically trained to identify reference questions such as, "Where are the non-fiction books?" and lead the customer to provide additional information: "I need materials on anatomy and physiology for assistance with my distance learning course." While the question is more than appropriate for a page to answer, pages should be trained to answer the question and then move the customer on to the reference staff for assistance with the request for specific materials.

Circulation Staff

Beyond basic skills, directional reference, and specialized training in customer interactions dealing with money, circulation staff need training in handling difficult customers as well as in advanced conflict resolution. In addition, they need the training of recognizing basic and directional questions that lead to reference questions. An additional area of customer service training for circulation staff includes how staff should handle questions that occur when no reference staff are on duty and how to verbally move between the roles of sometimes offering advanced service when no one else is there and sometimes not doing so.

Reference Librarians

Reference librarians need it all! By "all," we mean training in basic, advanced, and specialized service as well as handling money and conflict resolution. This employee group may have to support circulation and thus have to know reference specific customer service as well as serve as an ultimate authority in situations where there is no one to delegate to when the conflict or situation arises.

Volunteers

Volunteers need customer service training in general, to provide basic content to assimilate them into overall library commitment to customer service; then they need specialized training to address any unique volunteer responsibilities, such as

- Moving customers from one location to another in the library if the volunteer cannot meet their needs
- Learning basic library terminology to successfully assist customers
- Discovering what their roles and responsibilities are and are not in regard to serving library customers

Public Service Managers—Circulation and Reference

Managers need to have basic, advanced, and specialized skills as well as conflict-resolution skills. In addition, they need training in problem solving, as a mediator and, ultimately, an arbitrator or decision maker. Special skills are needed to investigate customer situations and to work on the task at hand of problem solving or decision making where a customer is concerned while taking care to support the circulation desk employees.

Upper-level Administrators

Typically, this group is the last in the chain of customer service transactions—and often administrators see only conflict transactions. Upper-level administrators must be cognizant of policies and procedures as well as all of the political ramifications of decisions made. Administrators need unique skills in gathering and assessing investigative data and in "closure," or in communicating to customers a finality in decision making.

Incorporating Diversity and Training

Before we move on to discuss how training can be tailored to match an institution's needs, we must pause to consider how diversity drives the training content. Although diversity is mentioned in many chapters throughout the book, the topic is important enough to clarify and summarize a variety of diversity issues for extraordinary customer service.

There are many definitions outlining what *diversity* means. When discussing the need to honor and respect all aspects of diversity, many managers now include aspects such as age, geographic, and gender differences and other aspects such as religion. For purposes of this discussion, however, diversity is defined as culture, race, and ethnicity.

Figure 2.2
Continuous Learning at Austin Community College

Austin Community College (ACC) offers a variety of learning opportunities for employees who need to learn customer service, basic and advanced technology skills, and other basic work-related skills. A highly decentralized environment, the college does not have many opportunities to bring all staff members together, but based on a critical need for consistency of operations. Typically, ACC:

- Chooses a focus for learning topics that revolves around a timeline, such as "spring/summer hot topics," "essential skills training," "excellent library service"
- Brands the learning period with a theme that includes a logo and phrase
- Designs a kick-off all-staff event with discussion of a values statement, the rationale, desired outcomes, individualized handouts, discussion of different learning styles and techniques and timelines
- Purchases and distributes advertising specialty items for distributing at kick-off and training
- Relates the activities to evaluations and evaluation timelines for the coming year
- Provides proctors for pre-assessment (does not include individuals who are staff members' managers)
- Provides multiple opportunities for learning, including online self-directed modules, video training, print "for dummies" instructions, teleconferences (if available), a learning partner, small-group learning or a class or larger-group learning
- Offers extended learning timelines during which no testing or assessment is done
- Offers multiple testing that includes employees taking a self-test prior to being assessed by managers

In follow-up discussions, employees have indicated that they prefer the flexibility of learning content, the extended timelines, and the variety of opportunities for demonstrating competence.

The many issues relating to diversity and customer service include diversity as it relates to library workers, volunteers, and internal and external customers. The issues include but are not limited to:

- Customers communicating in languages other than English need to be identified and addressed in customer service training.
  - How might library workers make customers feel welcome even though they do not speak the same language?
  - Can customer service training content include greetings and comments to lead customers to appropriate public service desks or to specific staff or volunteers?
  - What are the communication characteristics that are specific to certain languages that relate to customer service, such as do certain customers hesitate to approach people in authority? How might signage or initial contacts between customers and library workers assist in dispelling myths or realities?
  - Does the library have a "call list" for library workers, with names of those who speak languages or are skilled at greeting customers who do not speak English?
- Library workers themselves, both employees and volunteers, might not have complete command of the English language, including having lower literacy levels.
  - Are instructions for basic job responsibilities and core competencies in the language of the instructees and at appropriate reading levels?
  - Are job expectations relating to customer service clear about requirements and reading levels needed?
  - Is customer service training available for non-English speakers or for those with lower literacy levels? Are customer service workshops and—at the very least—customer service training content available in a variety of languages? Can content be available in a variety of formats for those who learn differently or for those with lower reading levels?
- Customer profiles—for customers of different backgrounds and with different languages—must be assembled for use in customer service training. Do they include customer expectations of service based on customer culture and/or ethnicity? Do they include specificity as to learning styles and reading levels based on diverse customers? Does content include recommended body language and techniques for making people successful?
- Customer service training should include information on avoiding language colloquialisms that are unique to a language or to sections of a country or state. Example:
  - The expression "looking things up" on the catalog is too vague and, for many languages, implies directions for looking upward. The phrase "finding books" on the catalog more easily translates.

In summary, managers must be careful to balance the identification of special issues and needs with the labeling of library workers or customers, which could create lower expectations. Managers must also be aware of the need to educate and "bring workers along" a continuum of learning extraordinary customer service that is up to library standards, not enable workers to remain at less-than-full participatory levels in the organization's customer service program.

3

Preparing Specific Training for Library Staff and Volunteers

Although customer service training content can be purchased, identified in professional training literature, borrowed from other profit and non-profit environments, or borrowed from all types of libraries, the best match of content to an institution's needs takes place by identifying good basic customer service content that matches your basic or general needs and then revising and customizing elements of that content or by specifically designing related content to meet your precise needs, especially those unique needs of your employees and volunteers.

Basic training needs that could be easily met and matched to generally and easily available content include:

- Telephone greetings
- In-person greetings
- Closure or exit information
- Basic assessments such as "Did you get what you need?"
- General positive language for customer/employee interactions
- Recommended language for possible negative or conflict interactions (such as fines, fees, security gate infractions)
- Employee/customer interactions for basic services such as basic reference questions
- "How to" use equipment/hardware such as copiers, scanners, self-checkout, printers, and keyboards and mice
- "How to" use basic software, for locating the library's homepage, customers accessing their library records, customers renewing books
- General employee/customer behavior interactions

Specific training needs that may need uniquely designed or customized content include:

- Telephone greetings for specific departments
- Telephone greetings for unusual situations, such as closures for weather conditions or facilities construction and remodeling
- In-person greetings for special-needs customers including for other languages/sign language, age-level greetings, differently abled customers
- In-person employee/customer service interactions for customers with needs, including other languages, different age levels, differently abled customers
- Advanced or in-depth reference and research interactions
- Conflicts with customers resulting from inappropriate customer behavior
- Basic information literacy interactions
- Advanced "How to" use equipment/hardware
- Advanced "How to" use software

Other areas of customer service training that require specialized, unique, or customized content are those for:

- Unique departments
- Unique job functions
- Special learning styles of employees
- Special preferences of employees

Reviewing Educational Profiles

These special or unique training needs requiring customized customer service content dictate that institutions create profiles of both employees and customers in order to match teaching and learning for customer service. These profiles—created for both employees and customers—are composed of general twenty-first-century characteristics or elements shared by most contemporary learners as well as specialized elements that are unique to individuals. Exploring aspects of general-learning profile elements and specific, individual-learning profile elements is critical to the success of both matching general customer service content and customizing or designing new content to meeting individual needs.

Profile Elements of Typical Learners

Today's learner has a profile comprising a set of characteristics and elements. This general profile must be studied by those critiquing general customer service content so that the delivery of content will be matched to the learning styles and preferences. Just a few of the characteristics and elements of the profile of today's learners follow:

- Are used to fast-paced activities
- Have shorter attention spans
- Need more "glitz" to both attract and keep their attention even for short periods of time
- Do not value or often are not aware of tradition and traditional ways

- Have different work ethics
- Work differently
- Are learning on the "surface" or are, often, learning just what it takes to get by
- Know popular culture and not culture
- Are not truly "self-directed" but are neither used to working nor know how to work with others or in teams
- Need frame of reference more often than not; that is, how does it relate to me/my job/my future?
- Want variety in learning opportunities...their learning styles are exacerbated by contemporary society
- Need continuous work on the development of their critical-thinking skills and therefore need extensive problem-based training
- Need lots of attention, assessment, and feedback

In addition to these general characteristics shared by most learners, individual employees will have elements of their learning profile that are specific to their situation. Factors that influence these specific learning profiles include the following elements:

- Experience prior to the current job
- Length of time at the job
- Experience at work
- Education
- Position responsibilities including supervision or coordination of other employees

Volunteers also will have learning profile elements that are specific to their roles as volunteers. Factors that influence volunteer learning profiles include the following elements:

- Work experience prior to volunteering in general as well as volunteering in your library
- Volunteer experience prior to volunteering in your library
- Education
- Unique competencies gathered through work and/or volunteer responsibilities
- Unique competencies through hobbies or other interests

Profile Elements of Typical Customers

While most people discuss customer profiles in relation to marketing strategies targeted to attract customers, customer profiles are also critical to identifying elements for creating basic and specific customer service programs. Profiles that are demographic or behavior-based assist managers in choosing elements of a library's customer service program (signage, ergonomics, facilities design, furniture arrangement) and customer service training content and how that content is packaged to train employees to serve customers.

Demographic profiles of customers outline life status, including marital, family, living arrangements; education levels achieved; learning preferences; learning styles; language preferences; income levels and likelihood of expending income on areas such as technology; work status, including types of employment and access to employment (travel to and from); and preferences such as reading likes and dislikes. Behavior-based profiles can be limited to behavior in general or behavior related to the library or information needs and can include visits to library resources (building or online), general or aggregate use of resources, and general or aggregate use of services.

Not all data can be easily gathered, however; much information to assist in compiling customer profiles is found in readily available aggregate sources such as census data, institutional data (in-person use and e-visit use) and umbrella institution planning data (such as county or city data), while other data are available through customer surveys and specific planning programs such as "Planning for Results." These profiles provide those designing the customer service program with information such as:

- Do customers live near the library, or do they travel distances for library services?
- What is the average educational level?
- What languages do they speak?
- Are customers entering in person, virtually, or digitally?
- Are customers returning, first-time, or infrequent users?
- Are customers—given their work and home time profiles—able to spend time "in the library," or is speed important in serving them?

With this data in hand, customer service greetings can be scripted, self-directed user interfaces can be designed, and signage and ergonomics can match customer needs. For example, libraries have chosen a more detailed library-information e-phone greeting when it has been determined that customers use the phone frequently *before* coming to the library. Library signage and information literacy elements (pathfinders, bibliographies, Web pages, and so forth) can be in a variety of languages when profile data indicate that library community members either use or prefer native languages.

When profile data indicate that customers define themselves in certain ways (such as by occupation or age) and use the library's Web site often, libraries can design user interfaces that allow the customers to find "themselves" on the front page with links to resources by type of customer such as "bestsellers for adults," "recommended resources for new parents," or "library resources for educators." All of these elements are critical to the design of the customer service program.

Matching Content to Context

Developing a table such as the following will help clarify the process of matching customer service materials to the context in which they will be used.

	Figure 3.1 Profile Elements for Designing Scripts	
Content	**Employee Profile Elements that Dictate Customized Content**	**Customer Profile Elements that Dictate Customized Content**
In-person greetings	Employees at the circulation desk do not have experience working in busy public service environments prior to coming to the library. Since they are not experienced in welcoming or greeting customers, managers select and customize customer service content in scripts for the most simple greetings. Volunteers are not experienced in working public service desks in busy public service environments.	The majority of customers are identified as having a variety of cultural and ethnic backgrounds. In-person greeting scripts are written in a number of languages and include both formal and informal greetings in requisite languages.
Conflicts with customers over fines and fees	Employee and volunteer learning preferences include learning within their work context. Employee and volunteer learning styles are primarily visual. Training in handling customer conflict is designed to take place at a circulation desk/appropriate public service desk with a short introductory movie and then role-playing with employees and volunteers assuming roles of both customers and employees.	Customer profiles include identification of issues relating to cultural and ethnic background and reticence to question authority. Customer service interactions concerning fines and fees include establishing parameters to provide customers with a variety of payment plans.

With this employee and volunteer data in hand, customer service training scripts can be designed and methods of delivery training can be offered to meet employee and volunteer needs and to match employee and volunteer learning styles and preferences. For example:

- Libraries may choose to provide more scripts rather than offer general training because data show that employees and volunteers at circulation or other public service desks are often uncomfortable with the difficult situations that need specific, consistent wording.
- Employees have indicated they like to learn through viewing others, so examples of how to handle Web access violations are provided both in written case methods and in video clips to offer two ways for employees to learn how to handle these situations.

Tailoring Training to the Library Environment

Additional profile characteristics and elements include identification of the type of work environment, the size of the overall work environment, and the specific elements of the narrower or more specific work environment, such as the department, and whether or not the customers being served are only internal or both internal and external.

Type of Library

Types of libraries are each "unique environments" and include public, academic, school, and special library environments. In addition to these environments, hybrid environments to be included for unique curricula are areas that combine two different types of libraries, such as joint-use facilities, and libraries "within" other libraries, such as the art departmental library within the college or university library that identifies itself as a special library. What makes these environments unique and different from one another is, obviously, the collection, but more important, the customers and, specifically for this discussion, the type and level of customer services that customers in each type of library receive and the profiles of these customers.

PUBLIC

Public libraries typically provide customers services and resources to support customers in meeting their educational, recreational, informational, and cultural needs in the form of reference services, materials to meet their needs, and programming. Public library customers can be all ages and from all backgrounds, with the most varied needs imaginable. Their needs can be short-term or long-term. Given these diverse needs, well-defined customer profiles are difficult to articulate for anything other than basic and short-term services or in communities with more homogeneous populations by either race or age. But even in these communities, customers will typically be from various backgrounds, with differing levels of educational attainment and different needs and expectations for library service. Employees and volunteers may have unique expertise in a variety of areas to assist in providing extraordinary customer service, and this expertise comprises elements of employee and volunteer profiles. It includes—to name but a few areas—knowledge of developmental stages of young customers; changing learning styles and preferences of older Americans; skills in other languages, including sign language; and awareness of the unique aspects of different cultural and ethnic groups.

ACADEMIC

Academic libraries typically provide services and resources to support customers in meeting their educational and informational needs in the form of reference services, materials to meet their needs, and some programming. Academic library customers are primarily adult, and their needs match both general and advanced study, basic and advanced work for specific disciplines, and in-depth research. Their needs can be short- or long-term. Customer profiles can be designed for basic and short-term services and for long-term services. Unique expertise of customer service profiles of the academic library employee include in-depth discipline knowledge to assist customers in special needs and in-depth research, advanced education to match customer education levels, and experience with levels of customers, such as first-generation college students.

SCHOOL

School libraries typically provide services and resources to support customers in meeting their educational and informational needs in the form of reference services, materials to meet their needs, and some programming. School library customers are the school population, and their needs match both general and advanced study, basic and advanced work for specific disciplines, and in-depth research. Their needs can be short-term or long-term. Customer profiles can be designed for basic, short-term, and long-term services. More and more, however, student families and, in some cases, community members use school libraries and must be included in profiles of library users. The developmental stages of young library users are among the key elements of the expertise of school library employees and volunteers in developing customer service profiles.

SPECIAL

Special libraries typically provide services and resources to support customers in meeting their informational and sometimes educational needs in the form of reference services, materials to meet their needs, and some programming. Special library customers are the population of a business or organization, and their needs match both general and advanced work, basic and advanced work for specific product or business needs, and in-depth research. Their needs can be short-term or long-term. Customer profiles can be designed for basic, short-term, and long-term services. Unique expertise of customer service profiles of the special library employee include in-depth product knowledge and knowledge of research needs of customers.

Size of Library

The size of the library (physical space or number of staff) matters greatly when planning for superior customer service, and sizes can dictate levels of customer service. For example, signage in a smaller library environment is usually limited. Staff and/or volunteers often have to provide more directional reference if orientation signage is not available.

Smaller library facilities offer fewer points of customer service contact; therefore, an information desk *and* a reference desk might not be possible. Staff and/or volunteers at one service location may well need to provide information and reference customer services all at one location. Close service points—such as a circulation desk very near a reference desk—dictate different service interactions to, for example, move customers among services. Lack of space for service points for each service population or discipline area means that adult services staff must assist younger customers, or general reference and in-depth subject-specific reference is offered at only one service point. Staff and/or volunteers at one desk may need much broader training, including a wide variety of customer profiles and a variety of scripts to meet both general and specific needs.

Department of the Library

No matter the size of the library, the existence of a department or the lack of that department necessitates changes in customer service approaches. For example, a lack of a young adult department means that all other service desks must have training in working with young adults; or, similarly, media or government documents departments being integrated into general collections means that subject and format-specific training has to occur with staff at general reference desks.

Internal versus External Customers

Traditionally, "internal" customers refers to those within the organization, as opposed to members of the public, or "external" customers. In this instance, however, we are thinking of internal customers as the primary client base that is local to a library jurisdiction and external as being those customers who are nonlocal and, thanks to electronic networks, can be anywhere in the world.

The broader the customer base, the more diverse customer service training is needed, and whether or not the broader base is brought about owing to diverse delivery formats or expanded use of heretofore limited services, customer services must be redefined to further specify customers for expanded profiles and service design. Examples include:

- A rich Web site with local and global customers means that customer service training goes beyond local customers and local-customer profiles. Often, local customers are considered internal to the mission of the library, while nonlocal, or external, customers are those not specifically included in the library's mission but clearly needing customer service.
- Libraries with specific customer populations such as special or academic library populations or even school library populations often find that when services expand beyond the library owing to partnerships or cooperatives, customer services need to change to meet external customer service needs.

Understanding employee and customer learning styles and preferences and matching teaching styles to learning styles and preferences are critical to the success of the extraordinary customer service program. It is possible to generate profiles for general users to provide data to create great customer service; that is, even though it is not possible to profile individual customers for specific-to-the-individual customer profiles, in general libraries can:

- Study general user profiles for twenty-first-century customers to determine general preferences for learning (for example, shorter messages)
- Assess census data content for relevant demographic information (such as education levels) to design appropriate signage, information literacy, and Web interfaces
- Become familiar with general population reading levels for signage
- Become familiar with general language vernacular to use in customer service for avoiding library phrases that are unfamiliar to the public
- Assume general levels for writing content and instruction for library users (such as designing instructions in middle-grade levels reading levels for general reading ease)
- Provide content in a variety of formats to meet diverse learning preferences (such as video streaming information literacy instruction on the Web site instead of just text)

Respecting Environmental and Organizational Constraints

Managers desire flow in their organizations, whether it is flow of employees and customers in and among furniture, hardware, and services or the flow of employee training and related policies and procedures.

Physical Layout and Customer Service

Library floor plans must be given great attention so that the best possible use of furniture and space is made to match customer profiles in order to enhance customer service. Layout should include attention to:

- Good ergonomics for customer flow
- Full ADA (Americans with Disabilities Act) compliance with special attention to profiles of special-needs customers
- Colors designed to prepare customers for services to match spaces (for example, calming colors for research and study areas, active colors to move customers quickly through circulation and check-out areas)

Unusual designs, difficult-to-navigate physical facility or furniture layout are profile elements demonstrating that simple general customer service directions need to be customized and scripts need to be customized to match services as customers are assisted or moved among customer service points.

Union versus Nonunion Shops

Organizations that provide additional structure and parameters to staff may well need special consideration for customer service profiles and training. Union contracts may address orientation, training, and education to provide standards for offering content and delivery. Union contracts might need great specificity to require management to meet employee needs for ensuring maximum employee success in the performance of their critical job functions. This specificity may include:

- A requirement for training to be provided in the widest variety of delivery formats
- Diverse content to meet special language, ethnic, or cultural diversity
- Varieties of time-of-day offerings to provide maximum opportunities to employees who maintain a variety of work shifts
- Required point-of-use training at employee work sites or workstations, instead of classroom or large-group activities
- Maximum possibilities for learning and testing for content mastery

Union organizations often handle training and education in customer service differently. For example:

- Union contracts may address initial training for employment and continuing education in a different manner, such as by limiting the amount of required training and education.

- Union contracts may seek more structured scheduling of training, such as "on work time" or by location, requiring that training be "at the location of the employer."
- Union negotiations may include discussions of customer service, such as techniques for handling customer complaints and grievances.
- Union discussions may include recommendations for requiring or not requiring scripts or specific language for assisting in customer interactions.

Unions may also want to address how management responds to those workers they consider to be "untrainable." In any environment, it is unrealistic to expect that all employees will be equally enthusiastic about all training content, including customer service. It is the responsibility of managers, however, to make it clear from job advertisements, job descriptions, interviews, first-day and first-week orientations, managers' performance expectations, and any probationary-period training what customer service training expectations are in place for all library workers. Part of the process of bringing employees around to seeing the value of customer service training is to see how the training relates to the organization's commitment to and requirements for training. At the very least, as it relates to training and customer service, employers should convey:

- Clear organizational vision that includes training commitment and commitment to extraordinary customer service
- Integration of training commitment and commitment to customer service into all documents that relate to all library workers
- An expectation to all library employees that training is not a choice but a job requirement.

Employees who do not meet these expectations of their job responsibility need to be managed as any employees who refuse to learn any other aspect of their job. Such employees should be subject to the same review stages and opportunities to correct their behavior as for any other issue, including appropriate documentation, verbal warnings, informal and formal meetings with written follow-up, formal warnings, disciplinary meetings and documentation, and probation or termination. While these processes will probably be mediated and reviewed by union representatives, employers who document expectations and employee performance will be better able to ensure that employees are held to organizational standards for customer service.

Managers should also determine how volunteers and customer service issues "relate" in union organizations. Issues can include:

- Are volunteers allowed—based on contracts—in public service areas providing customer service?
- If volunteers are allowed to provide customer service, are the standards and therefore education and training different for volunteers?
- Does the contract allow for volunteers to be trained alongside staff?

Organizational Structure

The organization of employees must be taken into account when planning for customer service. In more typical organizations, for example, who is responsible for what customer service area of training and delivery is clearly defined. For those in alternative structures such as matrix management organizational structures, multiple managers may have diverse, or even clashing, customer service requirements.

In addition, the growing number of remotely managed environments dictates an even greater variety of delivery formats needed for customer service such as in-person versus online service scripts and techniques for handling conflicts or special-needs requests online rather than in person. Clearly, individuals either using library services or resources or working to serve customers remotely also need training delivered in a variety of ways and have different profiles from "in-person" customers or employees.

Organizational Culture

The culture of an organization is basically the personality of the organization, and it includes the assumptions, values, norms, and signs or artifacts of employees and their behaviors. Nonprofit environments exhibit different cultures from profit environments, and many organizations exhibit, specifically, customer service culture.

Deciding on the Time to Train

When you train is a key question, and the answer is "continuously." To be an effective agent in changing employee behavior, managers should encourage employees to pursue training at every opportunity. Recommendations for continuous learning, training opportunities, teaching and learning processes, and the appropriate moments for teaching include:

- *Immediately.* Job descriptions, job advertisements, and interview schedules for bringing in new employees should include, as appropriate, the organization's commitment to customer service and management expectations for customer service behaviors as well as training and education. Interview questions should address specific customer service assessment, including attitude and commitment to quality customer service; knowledge, including positive language wording and knowledge of profiles; and skills and abilities, including scenarios for potential employees to respond to regarding preferred customer service behaviors.

  Volunteers should also be educated as to the organization's customer service commitment and immediately trained to provide a frame of reference for service and illustrate standards of service. In addition, managers need to determine volunteer customer service competency levels upon first "hire" to determine education and training needed and prior to putting volunteers on public service desks.

- *Within the probation period.* Orientation (first-day, first-week, and first-month) training and any other probationary-period training and education should include those critical elements of required customer service. Just as employees learn the collection or the processes and procedures critical to basic work flow, they should also be introduced to the customers for whom they are responsible.
- *Ongoing or point-of-use.* The organization and delivery of library training content should be designed to deliver point-of-use or immediate information training as well as provide longer-term or more educationally oriented knowledge-based curriculum.
- *Ongoing continuous improvement.* Using meetings (staff meetings, content meetings, decision-making meetings) is an excellent way to gather data on what is going on in the area of customer service delivery as well as the best way to fully integrate it into the organization. "Customer service" as an issue to be discussed should be on every general management agenda so that employees can share issues and answers and management can reinforce expectations for ongoing extraordinary service.
- *Special event.* Special event training such as all-staff training days emphasizes the importance managers put on customer service. All staff-development days should include some element of customer service, if only to assess the need for updating scripts, and discussion of common but new issues such as "all circulation desk people are getting more challenges on incorrect fines assessed. New scripts for handling this conflict need to be designed and integrated into the customer service curriculum.
- *Content continuously delivered.* Curricula for staff training days should provide the diverse delivery available throughout the entire training and education program; however, it should offer self-directed or reflective learning opportunities, group work of educational presentation with possibilities for discussion, and active learning in small groups. All curricula should include discussions of overall institutional commitment, management expectations, and standards of service excellence.
- *Annual.* Performance evaluations must include both a general discussion of customer service behaviors and specific feedback on whether employees measure up to standards and management expectations. If organizational performance evaluation forms do not provide specifics on customer service, then managers should identify areas of performance evaluation that specifically relate to customer service. Such areas may include "communication," as well as those areas such as "planning" that are not as specific but can take into account customer service concerns in the manner of "Are employees writing goals relating to customer service?" Also important is "professional development" or "staff development," which can include "Are employees and volunteers participating in required customer service training and education?"
- *Sporadic offerings.* On-site seminars, tutorials, and speakers and online training methods offer only sporadic training; however, they are recommended

because they provide on-the-job training or workstation or desktop training, which are considered some of the best ways to deliver critical training, since they are "point-of-use." Off-site training opportunities such as at conferences and workshops offer opportunities to explore benchmark external customer service practices to emulate or "how others do it 'good.'"

Spelling Out the Specific Needs of Volunteers

Volunteers play a variety of vital roles and are responsible for a critical array of work responsibilities in today's libraries. These volunteer work responsibilities can range from basic support to advanced, ongoing support of core work responsibilities. Whether volunteers complete the simplest of tasks or the most advanced and complicated work, the reality is that volunteers must be considered part of the workforce, and, as such, must be trained, developed, and educated in many competency areas and, most certainly, in any customer service training.

There are a variety of issues, however, concerning training and continuing education for volunteers, and they include both "opportunities" and "threats" in managing this important part of the workforce.

Volunteer Expectations

Volunteers arrive at the library with dramatically different expectations for work. Just like any employee, some volunteers are interested in being trained for and limited to narrowly defined, specific work responsibilities, while others seek broad work assignments, which naturally require broad training. Although training and education for volunteers *should* be matched to primary job assignments, integrating volunteers into all training required for excellent customer service training and education should be pursued by libraries and all library workers. Volunteers, however, might not be interested in or expecting extensive or ongoing training beyond training for primary work responsibilities. In addition, many volunteer jobs are not primarily public service positions; therefore, managers should expect to address and possibly change volunteer expectations that do not include customer service as valued, or even appropriate, training and education.

Management Expectations

Managers expect all employees and library workers to value library customers in general as well as training and education in general. It stands to reason, therefore, that managers expect all those in the workplace—in this case, volunteer workers—to value customer service training, to have a commitment to serving customers with the best possible service, to be motivated to expand beyond standard customer service business practices, to be aware of and exhibit the characteristics of professionalism in dealing with customers, and to maintain positive morale levels during the diverse aspects of customer interactions. Managers, however, must communicate their expectations—preferably through specific standards, written statements, and guidelines that govern volunteerism in the library. These expectations need to be integrated into management documents that concern and are made available to volunteers.

Managing Volunteers

Most manuals and guides concerning the management of volunteer services recommend that, no matter the size of the library, volunteer management come through one specific manager or coordinator. This method provides for consistency of all activities relating to volunteers, including the coordination of all training and education. One manager offers the organization to ensure that all volunteer workers are trained and educated initially and consistently as needed and that customer service content is appropriate to volunteer/customer interactions and responsibilities. Volunteer coordinators often play their most important role in balancing—for volunteers—their work responsibilities and the identification of what volunteers do not do in the workplace. It is often challenging for volunteer coordinators to have to explain that, although basic and often advanced customer service training is required by volunteers, not all customer interactions are appropriate for volunteer work responsibilities. Volunteer coordinators should be involved in the selection and assessment of customer service training content and should be seeking content that offers examples of how a customer/worker interaction might be handled one way by a library volunteer and another way by a library employee.

Selecting and Hiring Volunteers

Volunteer job ads, job descriptions, guidelines, standards, interview schedules, and assessment of successful "applicants" for selection should include terminology and phrasing that address management expectations for volunteers for initial and ongoing customer service training—no matter a volunteer's specific job. Interviews should then be prepared to articulate why and how often training will come into play for potential volunteers, stressing the importance of this area of library service and training. The terminology and phrasing used throughout volunteer management documents and the volunteer process itself should be consistent.

Additional Training Considerations

Issues relating to volunteer customer service training and education include learning styles, communication, cost of training in general and cost of training volunteers, keeping track and record keeping, and public relations. These areas, not unique in library management in general, often have unique aspects as they relate to volunteers.

LEARNING STYLES

Just as managers need to be aware of the learning styles of their employees, they should also be aware of the learning styles of their volunteers. This knowledge provides the foundation for the design of training and education in all areas, and specifically customer service, including the selection of basic and advanced content. Given the understandable lack of availability of many or most volunteers and the possible infrequency of work shifts, the match of style to content is a critical step. In addition, there is a need to provide training at wide varieties of times of the day and days of the week; therefore, learning styles must be carefully considered when matching presentation and teaching styles to learning styles.

COMMUNICATION

Maintaining standards of communication among employees is challenging. Keeping up with diverse schedules, hours of staffing, and numbers of staff is always time consuming; therefore, ensuring that volunteers are looped into the communication processes is often very difficult, but it is critical. Although good communication is crucial to the success of most aspects of the organization, communicating to volunteers about rapidly changing areas such as changing customer profiles, changing services provided to customers, and facilities issues affecting customer services and use.

COSTS OF TRAINING

Actual costs, in kind costs, and the costs of management time, such as planning time, and actual training time for training and education of library employees is expensive. While integrating volunteers into training programs adds to this cost for certain critical areas such as customer service, it is a necessary venture. Specifically, volunteers need to be figured into the customer service training budget for "time spent" (when volunteers are receiving training instead of completing work responsibilities), presenter costs, costs of handouts, content costs, and any travel costs.

RECORD KEEPING

Related volunteer customer service training includes training for volunteers who serve the public, and it includes record keeping for customer service interactions. Although at first glance keeping track seems easy, record keeping designed to assist in the completion of goals and outcomes relating to customers and customer service delivery is often detailed. Managers should ensure that record keeping is part of the job description of volunteers and that this critical area is also part of initial orientation and ongoing training and education.

Fundamentals of Customer Service Training for Volunteers

Just as the identification of customer service is recommended as a core competency for library employees, customer service should be on every volunteer's first day and first week training list. This list should be in the volunteer guidebook training materials and includes:

- The vision and mission of the organization
- The values of the organization

- The organization's commitment to extraordinary customer service for external customers
- The organization's commitment to extraordinary customer service for internal customers
- The definitions of external customers
- The definitions of internal customers (other employees of the umbrella organization [city, county, school, company, college, and so forth], all library employees, all volunteers in the umbrella organization, all volunteers in the library)
- How volunteer jobs interact with customers
- Any volunteer job descriptions
- Any management expectation lists for volunteers (this document might have to illustrate the reason for this customer service training requirement, since it may not be as clear to volunteers who "sign on to do a simple or little job" in the library)
- Any scripts appropriate to volunteer work responsibilities
- The volunteer evaluation form and how it addresses customer service expectations for volunteers

Ongoing Training and Education

Volunteer job descriptions should have similar language to employee job descriptions regarding the organization's commitment to continuous learning and ongoing training and critical customer service work responsibilities. Summary content—or titles of curriculum with timelines—adds clarity to the discussion of what role volunteers play in customer service. This summary content can be linked to specific volunteer duties. For example, a training plan linked to primary job responsibilities might outline the internal customers volunteers may work with on a project by stating, "Volunteers working with children's services on the production of crafts for after-school and summer club programs will be working directly with crafts materials but also with the children's librarian, a variety of internal personnel including other children's volunteers who are assisting in the delivery of the children's program, the Friends' member who handles the Friends' budget (for money for children's supplies), and the volunteer coordinator." This content gives the volunteer coordinator direction in what ongoing training might be needed for customer service and gives the volunteers a clearer understanding of how their "simple crafts and cutting-paper job" require them to work with other individuals in the library environment.

Volunteer Management in an "Extraordinary Customer Service" Environment

As extraordinary customer service content should be integrated into the content in all employee management information, it must also be integrated into all volunteer management information to ensure clarity of management expectations for these library workers. Managers should review all existing volunteer documents to assess the presence of customer service content.

- Assess your volunteer manual to make sure it includes content on customer service.
- Assess this manual to be certain it includes content on the organization's commitment to extraordinary customer service.
- Include definitions of customer service in all training content in general, as well as definitions of customer categories such as internal and external.
- Assess all documents related to volunteers (obviously including the volunteer manual) for inclusion of both volunteer and customer service content as well as a discussion or mention of volunteers and a commitment to their training including:
  - Job advertisements (reflecting desired qualities as an indication of the customer service orientation of the organization)
  - Job descriptions (indicating customer service as a stated component of the job)
  - First day/first week/first month training lists
  - Basic and advanced competency lists
  - Management expectation statements
  - Evaluation forms
  - Training information
  - Customer service content

Although many volunteers (and library employees) may think that introducing this level of training into "the life of volunteers" is not necessary, the reality is that volunteers need to ascribe to the basic tenets of the work environment, and including *all* library workers in training that insists on reasonable and equitable treatment of all colleagues in the workplace is a critical step in creating an environment where all individuals enjoy working.

4

Assessing and Anticipating the Needs of Customers

Librarians, especially public librarians, do not always think of themselves as teachers, but, of course, they are. School librarians play a significant role in K–12 teaching teams and see instruction as a major part of their job; teaching and instruction play significant roles in national and many state standards. Academic librarians are often faculty members of in their institutions and, if not, are considered partners in the teaching and learning process through both information literacy and classroom instruction. Consider for a moment just a few of the many ways in which public librarians at all levels are in the business of teaching, including presenting story hours, answering reference questions for point-of-use or one-on-one instruction, leading group tours (including classes) and small-group instruction (including classes), conducting readers' advisory services, offering information literacy classes in library computer labs, or providing ESL (English as a Second Language) classes or literacy tutoring sessions. Every day in myriad ways, librarians and library staff, in all types of libraries, conduct teaching programs for their public.

In light of how much training librarians provide for their clientele, it is somewhat ironic that library managers often automatically look to outside entities to provide training and development for their staff and volunteers. While library managers will always want to be aware of training opportunities offered through all formats of workshops, classes, conferences, and other outside venues, they have many internal resources available to teach their staff and volunteers and many long-term professional-development opportunities—as well as more short-term so-called teachable moments—to do so.

Maybe your first response to that statement is to think, "We talk to ourselves too much—we need to expose our staff to outside training so that they will bring back fresh ideas." We would never disagree that fresh ideas are important;

however, take a moment to ask yourself if you think there are customer service skills that you wish your staff had. We will assume the answer is yes, or you would not even be reading a book of this sort. So, what are they? By this point, you probably have a list; if not, make one. Then start to look down your list and think about what you and your managers and supervisors can offer in teaching your own staff and volunteers. You may surprise yourself with how much you have to impart to your own library workers before you have to send them to outside training oppotunities. And remember, outside training is a one-shot interaction, while what they can learn in-house is an ongoing tutorial. In addition, managers should always consider the appropriateness of assessing external training and professional-development program content and personalizing or internalizing ideas to create the perfect match for the institution.

This chapter will consider several specific techniques to provide and maintain continuous, or ongoing, in-house training in customer service skills. These include the following:

- Exploring scenarios for various types of customer interactions
- Using scripts to standardize excellent service and help staff through unusual, potentially stressful, or difficult encounters
- Designing and delivering content to assist staff and volunteers in understanding the distinction between policy and procedure
- Establishing expectations and outcomes for employee and volunteer customer service skills.

In many libraries, each of these methods can be developed in-house with expertise available from your management team. In some problematic cases, or perhaps in larger organizations, it may be necessary to bring in a consultant or other outside adviser to help establish a continuous learning training plan. However, this chapter is designed to convey ways to build what you already know about good customer service into a comprehensive and, most important, continuous plan for customer service improvement.

Identifying Potential Problems

One of the more popular teaching tools in management is the use of the "story" to illustrate a situation realistically and to apply content for the specificity that sets an issue in the context of the more commonly known environment. Stories can be cases, simulations or scenarios; however, scenarios lend themselves to training and work place learning because they are shorter in length.

Although scenarios can be used to teach the most critical interactions between individuals, they can present customer situations that are unusual, stressful, or particularly problematic. Scenarios as tools can serve the dual purpose of both making staff and volunteers feel more comfortable in their jobs and helping management gain more consistency and control over those situations. Thus defining those interactions that are unusual, stressful, or difficult is the first step in developing and then implementing those tools. Start to define those interactions by asking questions to gather information on critical issues as well as unusual or difficult issues.

- Do all staff and volunteers consistently greet the public in a welcoming manner?
- Do all staff and volunteers answer the phone in a consistent and courteous way?
- Is there a consistent procedure for handling multiple demands at public service desks?
- Do all staff know how to talk to the public about difficult policy issues?
- Does management understand which interactions make staff and volunteers most uncomfortable?
- What types of customer feedback channels are in place?
- Are data from customer feedback captured, analyzed, shared with staff, and acted upon?
- Do staff and volunteers know how to receive complaints from the public in a consistent and respectful manner?
- Do staff and volunteers have coping methods to help keep confrontational situations from escalating?
- Do managers and supervisors effectively communicate their expectations with library workers while supporting worker efforts to carry out management direction?

Your answers to these questions will drive your priorities as you decide how to focus your training effort. It is important to note that as you attempt to integrate a continuous process of improvement, all these considerations are interconnected. For example, if staff understand how to talk about difficult policy issues, they will be better able to receive the complaint in a respectful manner and keep confrontational situations from escalating.

Writing Scenarios for Particular Situations

Once the most critical areas of customer interaction have been identified, the first tool to use is a written scenario about how to handle specific situations. A scenario, the story set in the context of the organization, provides guidance to library workers on how to deal with these situations. It must be written carefully and used as a procedural document that should describe the situation, provide policy interpretation, and offer steps for handling the situation. The scenario should contain helpful phrases and elements of the scripts that the staff and volunteers can use in working with the public. Scripts written for use by volunteers should be written carefully to provide content for workers who may not have needed perspective from a specific educational background or previous training.

Clearly, all situations cannot be anticipated; thus it becomes necessary to distinguish among scenarios for difficult or critical *unusual* and *usual* situations.

Figure 4.1
Sample Scenario: Cell Phone Use

Because phones proliferate in libraries, the combination of creative ring tones and loud conversations threatens to disrupt the peace in the library. Staff and volunteers may find it difficult to approach customers to ask that they moderate their voices, especially when there may not be sufficient signage or even a policy specifically addressing cell phone usage. The following is a hypothetical example of a scenario for handling this difficult usual situation. In this case, while there is no specific signage or a library policy in place to prohibit cell phone usage, the library does have a disruptive-use policy that can be invoked.

Disruptive Use of Cell Phones

During an unusually quiet time in the library on Tuesday morning, a customer approaches the reference desk to complain that there is a customer in Leisure Reading talking—loudly—on her cell phone. The library worker thanks the customer for calling it to her attention, quickly saves her e-mail to "draft," and heads for Leisure Reading. As she reaches the area, she hears the customer conversing on the phone. Lowering her voice and catching the customer's attention, she approaches and asks the woman to politely lower her voice or continue the conversation outside. The customer indicates the need to continue for a minute; however, she does not lower her voice appreciably. The worker steps in a little closer and speaks a little louder, telling the customer that there have been a number of complaints and she needs to end the conversation or take it to the area outside the library. The customer indicates she will not be leaving or stopping the conversation, so the library worker states that she has no choice but to follow the steps in the library's policy manual and call the sheriff's office.

Additional training content to go with the scenario that outlines the context and presents the story is a list of recommendations and scripts or actual language to use.

Recommendations for Handling Cell Phone Issues

What the policy states: No policy prohibiting cell phone use in libraries. No specific signage. We do have a policy prohibiting disruptive use.

What you cannot do: ban the use of cell phones in the library

What you can do: enforce the disruptive-use policy

Remember to keep the following in mind in this and similar situations:

- Keep control of the situation by maintaining your composure and following through in an orderly and businesslike progression.
- Know your policies and procedures. If you make a threat (such as calling the police), follow through. Know in advance if the police will come. If they will not, then do not threaten to have the customer removed.
- Be sure the person is not a physical threat to anyone in the library, including yourself. If he or she makes threats, or displays any violent behavior, leave the situation and contact the police immediately.

Scripts for Handling Cell Phone Issues

This is the progression for enforcing the disruptive-use policy. First, approach the customer to politely say:

"Excuse me, Sir/Ma'am; your voice is disturbing other library users. Would it be possible for you to either lower your voice or continue your conversation outside?"

If he or she is reasonable, the situation will be diffused; if not, a follow-up is required:

"Sir/Ma'am, if you do not lower your voice, I am going to have to ask that you leave the library."

If the customer still does not lower his or her voice and does not go outside, you should follow up one one more time:

"Your voice is too loud, and I have asked you twice to lower it. I must ask you to leave the library at once."

"No way. I'm staying right here."

"In that case, I will have no choice but to contact the sheriff's office."

In using the scenario in training or in discussing an actual situation in the "customer service continuous learning" agenda item, managers should present the scenario, identify the salient elements and observations that can be made, discuss the overarching policies and procedures, identify the best language to use, and then establish the best language for future issues as well as actions that can be taken to improve this situation.

Similar scenarios can be developed for a variety of situations. Note that the scenario shown above contains not only policy guidance but also sample scripts to use with customers and instruction on how to handle the situation as the confrontation escalates. Keep in mind that these written scenarios are for use by library workers only and, unlike policy statements, need not be shared with the public.

Critical usual situations are those very important and typical interactions that set the tone of the organization and define often the first interaction workers have with customers. Difficult usual situations, those that arise on a regular basis—such as how to respond to complaints about customers viewing objectionable material on the Internet—can be handled with a precise scenario. In the case of difficult unusual situations, it should be sufficient to provide guidelines for how to handle the unexpected, including whom to call in case of an emergency.

In addressing difficult unusual situations, it is much harder to prepare the type of document we have included above for cell phone usage. Difficult unusual situations are difficult precisely because they cannot be predicted. But even the most difficult situation will fall into predictable categories. The following represent some—but certainly not every—category of difficult situations that might be encountered at any library. While most of these might be considered difficult usual situations, you could easily use these categories to prepare for those unexpected situations that will inevitably arise.

Unruly or Disruptive Behavior

- Loud talking
- Internet porn watchers and other bad online etiquette
- Rude behavior
- Misbehaving kids and teens
- People using the library to hold classes, conduct business, or other inappropriate use
- Unattended children and children left at the library at closing time

Overly Demanding or Unreasonable People

- The customers who want every rule bent for them
- The teachers who want extended loans
- The faculty who want to keep items in their offices
- People who work the system (in positive ways that maximize their use of available resources over multiple locations as well as in negative ways where they flaunt rules, exploit inconsistencies in staff practices, and circumvent established policies and procedures such as item limits or fees)
- Government officials or others in the organization (faculty, administration) who feel you work exclusively for them
- The person who wants to use interlibrary loan for fifty items at a time
- The customer that has ten books from this library, five from that one, and another two from the other; and some of them get renewed and some come back; she has three books waiting, and can she put that one back in rotation until she finishes what she has out? . . .

Customer Complaints

- "I definitely brought that back—you lost it!"
- "This letter from the collection agency is the first notice I got about this."

- "You sent me a letter on this, and I just went and checked, and there it was on the shelf."
- "What do you mean I can't stay late in the meeting room. I'm very trustworthy. I'll just lock up when I leave."

Reinforcing Scenarios with Role-playing

Once you have developed scenarios to control a few of the most problematic situations, you can begin to disseminate these to staff. It is important to have a core working group of library staff to either draft the scenarios or review them once management has drafted them. After they are vetted by library workers who work with the public on a daily basis, they can be reproduced and distributed. The scripts should be discussed with workers to be sure that they are comfortable with them, understand the policy issues involved, and will, in fact, be a tool that will be helpful with other staff members and with volunteers.

One very effective way to train library workers to deliver consistently high customer service, especially in difficult situations, is to conduct role-playing exercises. This can be done in formal and informal training situations ranging from library worker meetings to staff-development days to in-service workshops presented by library staff or outside trainers. Role-playing offers staff the opportunity to rehearse their scripts and their reactions in a nonthreatening environment where they can be coached and can refine their responses. Role-playing also allows staff to put themselves in the role of the customer. Being able to see the interaction from the customer's point of view and putting the customer's words in their mouths encourages staff to be more empathetic with customers' concerns.

Role-playing will seem stiff to many persons and, for that reason, they may be more fixated on the exercise itself than on the skills they are supposed to be learning. This distraction can be lessened with humor. For example, let staff have a little fun in exaggerating the customer's complaint or the specific situation. Another way to alleviate tension is for management staff to participate. Seeing managers participate may lend an aspect of humor to the situation and create a feeling that everyone is learning at the same time (and, it could be argued, management staff need the training as much as or more than other staff). One word of caution, however, regarding management participation in the role-playing exercise: given the staff situation, it might be advisable for managers not to play the roles of customers, thus intensifying the intimidation factor felt by the person playing the staff.

Role-playing can also be varied as a teaching technique:

- Library workers can read and discuss scenarios presented, then take part in role-playing characters from the scenario. (Scripts are then brought in after the role-playing to illustrate best practice.)
- Characters in role-playing—typically one type of personality—can be randomly assigned for acting out, or one type of staff member (if feeling comfortable) can be assigned roles antithetical to his or her personality.

Positive Language

While you cannot always anticipate every situation that arises, it is possible to provide training in approaches to critical situations as well as any situation that can be tense or even confrontational. As we will see later in this chapter, scripts work well in those situations that are predictable, but for situations that are more difficult to predict, it is still possible to give staff phrases that they can use in a variety of interactions with the public. These phrases are designed to calm, soothe, and relax customers in difficult moments and to diffuse situations that otherwise might turn unpleasant.

Whenever possible, the goal of any customer service interaction should be to turn a customer who is either already angry or about to become angry into a friend and ally. Specific examples of positive language phrases and sentences, as well as negative language to avoid, are provided in Chapter 1.

Employing Scripts for Common Concerns

One means of training and preparing library workers for positive customer service is to provide them with scripts to use in a variety of customer interactions. Many private-sector organizations use scripts to guide employees through exchanges. They are particularly useful in telephone contacts and with online interactions because they can be referred to without the customer being able to observe that the person is reading from a script. Scripts can also be helpful with in-person interactions, especially in helping staff to cope with difficult situations and to make certain that they deliver consistent service at those moments when they may otherwise neglect their customer services skills. They also help ensure that customers hear the right message and the same message across various staff and from multiple locations.

Scripts can provide staff and volunteers with the words to say at those moments when they are most likely to forget what to say. This will mainly happen when they are rushed or when they are facing a hostile customer. Predicting the types of interactions that can occur at these moments will help management staff decide where scripts can be helpful. The following are ideal situations for using scripts:

- Answering the telephone
- Placing telephone callers on hold, transferring calls, or returning calls
- Explaining library policies (especially the difficult or unpopular ones)
- Explaining library procedures (especially the difficult or unpopular ones)
- Responding to complaints, particularly about sensitive topics
- Talking to the media
- Taking requests for information from law enforcement agencies.
- And, in general, saying, "No" or "Stop" or "You can't"

Even the most routine of these situations can sometimes make the most seasoned veteran nervous, especially when one is rushed or otherwise tense. Scripts for these and other situations will provide staff with a valuable tool to help them more comfortably control public service interactions while providing consistent information to the public.

Although organizations should identify and design their own scripts, reviewing samples often sparks creativity and discussion. In the script below, while the language is critical to customer service success, the words and phrases in italics indicate those elements of an extraordinary customer service program.

For scripts to be effective, they must be carefully considered, simply constructed and consistently applied. This means that some thought and advance preparation need to go into the creation and distribution of scripts. The following tips will help:

- *Decide which interactions you want to script.* Not every conceivable interaction can be predicted and scripted. Workers will be confused—not to mention insulted—if you attempt to script many routine interactions. You may find that you want to confine your scripts to handling customers on the telephone and to a few high-stress moments when you want to help your staff stay cool under pressure and deliver the right answer.
- *Consult with frontline workers and middle managers.* This is one of the best ways to find out what scripts are most needed. Find out which situations make staff and volunteers most uncomfortable. One quick way to do this is to ask what library policies they most dislike. These are the policies about which they are most likely to tell a customer, "Yes, I know it's a terrible policy, but the administration makes us do it." Conversely, find out what policies workers find most agreeable. These are the policies about which they may be defensive, provoking such statements as "Most people find our meeting room policy very fair—yours is the first complaint we've ever had about it!"

Figure 4.2 Sample Script: Circulation Worker	
Customer to circulation worker	I want to use my USB port in the public workstation. Can you help me?
Circulation worker	I can't leave this service desk, but I can help you until the reference librarian is available. Some of the workstations do take USB ports and they are labeled on the left side of the keyboard. They should be—according to this floor map of the computers—the PCs numbered as 3, 4, 5, and 6. Go ahead and try it or wait by a workstation, and I will signal the reference librarian that you are waiting for assistance.
Customer	That's okay. I'll just wait by the reference desk so I don't miss them.
Circulation worker	That's fine. If you turn the half-page floor map over, there is an illustrated drawing of the keyboard and the monitor with simple instructions. That might provide you with additional information.
Customer	Thanks.
Circulation worker	Check back with me if you don't get the help you need.

	Figure 4.3 **Sample Script: Reference Staff**
Reference staff	Are you finding what you need?
Customer	No.
Reference staff	I'm sorry. Can I help you find something?
Customer	No.
Reference staff	I'm sorry we're not meeting your needs. I can find someone else to help or, if you decide you need help from me, let me know. Here is my card and I'm on the desk here for the next hour.
Customer	Thank you.

- *Write scripts carefully and with feedback from the library workers who will be using them.* Once you have decided which interactions to script, then write the scripts carefully, being sure to get plenty of feedback from your staff. Avoid investing too much pride of ownership in your script. Remember, it is an organic document that can change with experience and feedback from staff. If you have multiple outlets in your library, consider piloting the scripts in a couple of locations and see how they work for a few weeks.

- *Distribute scripts to library workers within a training context.* You should not simply write the scripts, hand them to staff and volunteers, and expect changes overnight. Scripts are only one of many tools to use in training others how to deliver excellent customer service. They should be introduced in a continuous-learning context that helps workers to understand how other factors affect communications, including nonverbal cues, tone of voice, mental attitude, and the effects of stress. This training context might be provided at a session of a staff-development day, at a manager's training session, or at a regular staff meeting. Role-playing exercises will help library

	Figure 4.4 **Sample Script: Children's Librarian**
Adult customer	(*Stepping in front of the child at the reference desk...*) I need help at the copier. Can you help me?
Children's librarian	I certainly can. I was just finishing up with this customer, and I can be there to help you in a few minutes.
Adult customer	My copies won't come out and I'm in a hurry.
Children's librarian	I understand. I can signal the circulation staff to help you until I get there.
Adult customer	Why can't you help me?
Children's librarian	I'm sorry, but I was already helping this customer. I'm almost through, so I can get someone to help you immediately or you can wait for me, but it will be just a few minutes if you need me to help you.
Adult customer	Never mind. If I can't get help from you, I'll just go to another desk.
Children's librarian	Again, I'm sorry I can't help you immediately. (*Librarian signals the circulation staff to go to the copier to assist. Depending on the discomfort or anger level, the librarian should complete an "accident form" or "customer support form," since the interaction with the customer did not resolve itself.*)

workers become more comfortable with the scripts and also help them learn the text.

- *Provide library workers with guidelines about when and how to use the scripts.* Scripts can be effectively used only with guidance from managers and supervisors. Be sure that all staff have the scripts and encourage them to ask questions and provide feedback. You should expect staff to find using a script in a conversation with a customer to be very awkward at first. Some staff and volunteers may feel that scripts are more of a nuisance than a help. Be patient in working with these scripts. On the other hand, to be sure that the scripts are being used, you might consider establishing with supervisors some expectations for the integration of the scripts into the workflow of their units. This is especially important—and easily observable—with telephone transactions.

- *Empower staff and volunteers to know when it is wise to depart from the script.* Because it is impossible to anticipate every reaction or statement that another human being will have, scripts can be effective only up to a point. Otherwise, you have to construct elaborate if/then scenarios, which can become complicated and confusing. Similarly, you cannot force any interaction into the confines of a known script. And remember that your staff are not acting in a play—they will need to ad lib most of their lines. What is most important is the spirit of the content of the script. Make sure that workers understand the underlying intention of writing a script in a particular way.

Now we will look at how to construct scripts in three situations.

Telephone Scripting

As shown in Figure 4.5, scripts can be of particular value when interacting with customers by phone. Because the public forms a lasting impression of the library through its initial interaction, it is important that the telephone exchange project an image of professionalism and service. This starts with the way in which the staff answer the phone. It is not too much to ask for everyone in the organization to answer the phone the same way, usually some combination of the name of the library and the individual's first name and some other added greeting, such as:

"Point Pleasant Public Library, Nancy speaking, how may I help you?" or "Good Morning. Washington Middle School Library. What may I do for you today?" or "Good afternoon. Reference Desk, River Bend Campus Library."

Just as with name tags, many staff are uncomfortable giving their names. Your library policy may allow staff not to use their names, and you can still fashion a welcoming message without them. What should be avoided is simply a statement of the organization name, and use of any informal shortcut, like "Library," should be avoided. Whatever you decide to use, however, you should script it and stick to it. But answering the phone is just the first step. Other telephone interactions that can be scripted include the following:

	Figure 4.5 **Sample Script: Complaint**
Customer	I want to complain about that circulation staff member over there. She was rude to me.
Reference staff	I'm sorry if our service did not meet your needs. Let's go where we can talk privately. (*Moves from the reference desk.*) Could you describe your interaction for me?
Customer	She was rude to me. She's always rude to me!
Reference staff	I need to follow up on this, and I need for my report to be specific. Can you give me some examples from today and from other exchanges? Can you give me very specific examples? In addition, following our discussion, you should feel free to complete this response card.
Customer	She treats me disrespectfully. She calls me by my first name, and she doesn't know me well at all. I am much older than she is! That's rude.
Reference staff	I hear what you are saying. Please understand that she did not mean this as a sign of disrespect. Our staff are trained to connect with customers by addressing them directly. Did you share with her in earlier discussions that you prefer to be called by your last name?
Customer	No, I didn't; but she should know!
Reference staff	I will let her know of your preferences.
Customer	Thank you. Maybe I should not have said anything but I want to.
Reference staff	I understand. I'll share this with the staff member. Thank you for coming in and sharing this with me. We want our customers to feel comfortable and to have a good exchange at all customer service desks.

- Placing the call on hold
- Transferring the call
- Taking information to call the person back
- Answering the "loaded" questions such as "When do you close?" for the phone call received thirty minutes before closing.
- Conducting a reference interview or checking to see if an item is in stock
- Answering basic library policy and procedure questions (hours of operation, how to get a card, directions, and so forth)

As with so many other aspects of customer service, train staff learning telephone etiquette to remember the golden rule: treat the customer as you like to be treated when you are a customer. We all have had the experience of calling a business, navigating maddening phone trees, being passed from one unhelpful person to the next, having to repeat the question over and over until we hang up with no satisfaction.

A few simple rules—built into your phone script—will help your staff provide consistently positive and helpful telephone service to your customers. Consider these points in developing your telephone scripts:

- Listen. Be sure you understand what the customers need. Do not assume you know what they need.
- Take notes if the question is complicated. *Script: "Thank you for your patience—I'm writing this down so I make sure I get all the details."*

	Figure 4.6 **Sample Script: Telephone**
Circulation staff answering the phone	Freeman Library. How may I help you?
Caller	What time do you close this evening?
Circulation staff	We close at 9:00 tonight, and we stop checking out materials at 8:45. You will need your library card and a picture ID. Remember if you need to copy materials, you'll need to get here no later than 8:30.
Caller	I'm going to be right there.
Circulation staff	Can I look up something for you before you make a trip? Or look up items to save you time?
Caller	No, thanks. I'll be there.

- Do not make customers repeat the reason they called. If you have to transfer the call, briefly relate the problem to the next staff person before you send the call through.
- Explain what you are doing. If you need to transfer the call, put the call on hold, or call them back, be sure to let the customers know what is happening, why, and how long it will take. *Script: "I need to put you on hold for a moment while I look that up. I will be back with you within five minutes. Are you able to hold?"*
- If you need to transfer the call to another person or department, explain why. Be sure to tell customers what to do if they get disconnected. *Script: "I am going to transfer you to our children's librarian. She is the best person to answer all your questions about the Summer Reading Program. If you get disconnected, please call me back at ___. My name is _____."*
- If you need to call back the customers, give an estimate of how long it will be. *"I am going to need to research your question and call you back. I will call you back by ___. I should have an answer by then, but if not, I will call and let you know how much longer it will be."* (And be sure to note when you said you would call back and actually call back within the time promised.)
- Give customers more than they asked for. If they ask, "What time do you close?" they really want to know if they can make it to the library before you close. *Script: "It's 8:30 now, and we close at 9:00. You'll need to bring your current library card and a photo I.D. and if you want to photocopy print items, print out resources, or duplicate tapes, you'll need to bring exact change and allow for at least one hour of time to complete your work."*
- When you complete a phone transaction, ask if you have answered the question. *Script: "Have I answered your question?"* This is a crucial step. Customers will often be reluctant to speak up and say that they have not been given the right answer, but if they are prompted, they may say, "Actually no, the question that I asked was ..."

Using the tools and techniques of scenarios, role-playing and, scripts in continuous learning for customer service permits a steady application of content to the organization and its typical and unique situations. In addition, these tools and techniques provide specific or exact wording to use in identifying outcomes, achieving consistency, and evaluating staff.

Distinguishing between Policy and Procedure

A critical aspect of continuous learning for customer service is the inclusion of customer service policy and customer service procedure. All training should distinguish between policies and procedures.

Policies are the foundation for doing business in the library. Policies should precede implementation or action. The word *policy* means different things to different people in different settings. In general, a policy is a guiding or governing principle. In the context of libraries or government entities, a policy is approved at the senior levels of the entity and:

- Is a governing principle that mandates or constrains actions;
- Has institution-wide application;
- Changes infrequently and sets a course for the foreseeable future;
- Helps define and ensure compliance, and enhances the institution's mission;
- By its existence as an "approved" statement of intent and commitment, reduces institutional risk.

Policies should be approved by governing bodies of organizations and by legal counsel (when applicable), continuously reviewed for currency and timeliness, supported by procedures that are reflective of contemporary need (examples: ADA, harassment), be used to inform others for proactive grassroots support, and answer the question "Why are you doing this?"

Policy language is consistent (among policies as well as within); clear, including who/what/when/where/how; directive (___ will/will not); specific (who is supposed to do what by title or position); reviewed consistently; "advertised" to encourage collective investment; legal when necessary; and based on research to identify benchmark and best practice. Policy language should not include numbers, have dates (except for the written/approved/reviewed date), be put in place without approval, be hidden, be created in a vacuum, or include names of people. Policies are considered "valid" if they comply with current laws and ordinances (local, regional, state, and federal), are reasonable, are fair, avoid denying based on unreasonable criteria, do not impose unreasonable penalties, and are nondiscriminatory. In addition, they should be applied equally, accessible and quantifiable, well written, displayed and easily assessed for infractions.

Procedures emanate from policies. They provide the how that corresponds to the why of policies. Although they also avoid names of individuals, they can include numbers, dates or timeline statements (for example, the end of the day), and the type and number of actions they perform. They are clear, simple, step-by-step instructions outlining how activities are performed.

Examples:

Policies

Policy: The library charges customers fines for overdue materials.

Procedure:

1. Customers present materials.
2. Materials are wanded in to the online system.
3. Online system assesses fees.
4. Fees are outlined for customer.
5. Customer is given a printed invoice.
6. Customer pays the fine.
7. Customer is given an invoice for the receipt of fees.

Policy: Use of cell phones is limited in the library.

Procedure:

1. Signage limiting use of cell phones is visible upon entering the library.
2. Customers place cell phones on "silent" upon entering the library.
3. Library workers inform customers of policy when asked.
4. Library workers notify customers when inappropriate use of cell phones occurs.
5. Library workers make every effort to correct inappropriate behavior but can call security when policy is violated.

The customer service policy outlines the libraries commitment to and general values guiding the library's customer service. It includes the library mission, or an intrepretation of the mission statement as it relates to customer service, and can also denote a general statement about fairness, courtesy, and respectful treatment of customers in providing the libraries services and resources. And it can also include expectations of customer behavior while using the library.

Policies can have statements illustrating behavior and can reference equity in access as well as any processes in place to establish an exchange of ideas on customer opinions and needs. Ethics statements should be included in customer service policies to provide a framework for both staff and customer behavior.

Examples of ethics statements that might be found in behavior and access sections:

1. Customers of the _____ Library are treated with equal respect, and requests are given equal importance in all aspects of public service.
2. Customers and customer interactions are given all appropriate courtesy, and staff will strive to be flexible in meeting customer needs.
3. Customer service procedures—and the policies that support them—are designed to provide equitable access to library resources and services.

Library rationale for policies and procedures is available upon discussion or challenge of services.

4. Customers are encouraged to provide feedback on the services and resources they receive.

Policy content on ethics should include content on equity in access, confidentiality of customer records, use patterns, and a statement on the definition of *children* and how their records are handled. The policy may refer to overriding legal documents such as the federal Patriot Act or state legislation. Policies may also include employee training standards in providing services regardless of their opinion or belief and may mention elements of what is handled in greater depth in the reference policy.

Procedures

Procedures might include:

- How customers are greeted
- How customers have fines and fees explained to them
- Specific techniques and scripted language on how customers are given information about federal and state legislation that governs access to and use of information
- Specific techniques and scripted language on how customers are confronted when charged (by another customer) with using inappropriate content
- Specific techniques and scripted language on how customers are confronted when found by library staff to be using inappropriate content

All types of libraries—within the parameters of their own organization or umbrella institution—need to write policies and procedures that provide service but allow for flexibility regarding individualized judgement calls for customers or situations. Terms that can be inserted that allow for flexibility include: *whenever possible, using judgment,* and *allowing for unique aspects of the situation.*

There is one more key distinction between policies and procedures that can be helpful in customer service training of staff. Because policies are created and adopted by management in partnership with the administration, the umbrella organization, and advisory or governing boards, they are not changeable by staff. On the other hand, procedures are often within the prerogative of some level of staff member to change without going back to the governing board for approval. This distinction is important because it provides staff a key guideline in what to say to customers. Many times a customer might demand that a library employee temporarily change or suspend a policy that they disagree with. Staff can be provided with scripted language to respond to such demands in a way that politely but firmly states to the individual that the policy is adopted by the governing body and that library staff do not have the power to change it. This can be followed up with offering to convey the customer's desire that the policy be changed to the governing body or requesting that the customer complete a customer service suggestion or complaint form. As we have said, however, staff may have areas over which they can exert flexibility or judgment. Managers must identify parameters for staff so that they feel empowered to make allowances that are appropriate and permissible.

In light of this exchange, you could devise a script for staff and volunteers something like that presented in Figure 4.7.

In this situation, the policy is not changeable by the employee, and that knowledge removes the employee from further conflict with the customer. The procedure—the amount of time that customers have on the computer—is within the employee's control, and she or he can offer flexibility in that situation. In addition, the customer service program allows for communication about services to provide avenues to management, and these avenues allow employees to feel comfortable when managers are not present. Library workers' knowing what they can and cannot change is the first step in empowering them to respond to customer requests and concerns.

Anticipating Problematic Circumstances

Library staff and volunteers, when appropriate to their position, need to be hired based on their knowledge of general customer service standards of excellence, their customer service experience, and their commitment to the organization's customer service standards.

The Interview

The organization's interview process should include questions, and possibly scenarios, on the treatment of customers.

Figure 4.7 Sample Policy versus Procedure Script	
Customer	I am so frustrated.
Library staff	I'm sorry to hear that. How may I help?
Customer	You can start by kicking these kids off the computer. They are only playing games. I need to get on and check my e-mail, and I never have enough time to do that.
Library worker	Well, according to library policy set by our [administration or city council or county commissioners], we don't restrict children from playing games on the computers.
Customer	But I think you should. You allow us to have only 30-minute sessions, and that is never enough time.
Library worker	I understand your frustration. There are a couple of things I can do for you. First, I will be happy to record your complaint and forward it to our library director so that she can consider your objections and share them with the council. You can also take this suggestion form with you and return it at your leisure. Second, if there is no one waiting, I can extend your session to give you a little more time to work. Third, I can see if it is possible to identify another computer in our [name another area of the library] area to free up so that you don't have to wait.
Customer	Well, that is very accommodating of you. Thank you.

1. Give an example of language you might use when you are assisting customers who are reaching your service point after waiting in line for an extended period of time.
2. How would you approach a customer who is hitting or being rough with a public service printer?
3. How would you answer this customer's question: "Why do I have such a large fine? You waived the fine of the person in front of me? Why aren't you waiving my fine?"

Orientation

New employees have a wide variety of areas to be included in their "day-one" orientation, however, customer service elements of day one should include awareness of copies of any policies and procedures and accompanying scripts that are derived from legal documents (for example, access, viewing) and customer greetings. "First-week" training information should include a discussion on management expectations of customer service (policy, any additional statements), an observation of positive customer service interactions (either in-person or role-playing), and a tour of the library's customer service content and such policies, procedures, scenarios, scripts, and processes that staff and volunteers can use on topics such as peer training and online interactive resources. Managers should not expect workers to end their first week trained, but by that week, new workers should know that there is a policy, as well as the most salient and legally critical aspects of the policy, and they should have observed good customer service and have planned, with their managers, when they will take the training the library provides. In addition, managers training new workers in customer service should provide copies of evaluations that make reference to customer service expectations and evaluation.

After the first month, library workers should be knowledgeable about the policy, should have followed good behavior, should have been observed in the workplace exhibiting good customer service behavior, and should have received the basic training required of new employees and volunteers. Managers should also check with peers, if available, for any observations and should review the customer service feedback mechanisms to see if any new workers are mentioned. Managers should take care to:

- Not "throw" staff or volunteers on the public service desks with minimal training and, if it is necessary, should tailor training to on-the-job training and be flexible in observing success
- Identify new workers as trainees to inform customers that the employee is in a learning mode
- Give immediate positive and negative feedback

After one month—or the timeline designated between worker and management—new workers should be able to meet basic standards of customer service. Organizations should plan training following the first month to coincide with the organization's probationary periods. If there is a six-month probation, basic and advanced customer service training should be completed by the end of five months and observation, correction, improvement, and evaluation opportunities should be established.

Customer Service Evaluation

Worker evaluation mechanisms might (and should) include specific questions on customer service, but if managers are working within general evaluations they should seek sections that can serve as umbrella categories, such as "quality of work" and "communication."

Judgment:

> *Does the employee exhibit good judgment in customer-service interactions?*

This question is then accompanied by a Likert scale response such as:

_____ The library worker follows the organization's customer service scripts for assisting users.

_____ The library worker does not use the scripts for customer service but has positive interactions through the use of similar language.

_____ The library worker does not use the scripts for customer service, and there have been customer complaints from interactions.

> *Does the employee exhibit strong communications skills?*

The worker's communication skills are excellent, good, acceptable, not acceptable, not applicable.

Manager comments—after checking "good"—could include: *"The library worker communicates well with customers using the organization's scripts."*

In summary, scenarios, role-playing, and scripts provide basic, ongoing, and advanced opportunities for continuous learning of customer service. This content, either general or personalized to meet specific organizational needs, provides staff, volunteers, and managers with significant tools with which to continuously train and evaluate the critical employee-to-customer interaction that is so vital to the success of the twenty-first-century public, school, academic, or special library.

5

Tracking and Responding to Customer Feedback

How do you know if your organization is effective in serving its customers? You ask your customers and, of course, your library workers as well. Feedback is the critical link in providing excellent customer service and in training to provide extraordinary service. As customers ourselves in other businesses, organizations, and markets, we all know the many ways that others ask for feedback: print or online customer response cards; follow-up surveys (phone, print, and online); workers' (in break rooms) and customer suggestion boxes; customer and staff complaint forms; in-person "clipboard" surveys for exiting customers; focus groups for library worker or customer; public service/worker dialogue (called "questioning") to include requests for customers to participate in response programs and scripts; forms and processes for public service staff and volunteers to systematically capture verbal customer comments in online or print, by writing/response or by fax or telephone. But what happens to all those comments? Who processes all that feedback? In businesses and organizations that are serious about excellent customer service, the information goes back to management, is assessed for relevance, is integrated into the customer service program, is "answered" when questions and comments warrant responses, and, in general, is shared with public service employees and, where applicable, umbrella organizations or upper-level administration. In highly effective organizations, feedback information is shared with library workers at all levels.

While staff and volunteers can be given numerical data, raw numbers often will not tell the whole story. The data must be organized, interpreted, and specific. Also, data must be combined with both anecdotal and narrative feedback to put the customer experience in human terms. Other sources of information also contribute to the effectiveness of customer service effort, including service data (use of services) and benchmarking data (comparing your organization with others or with your own services at a specific point in time). And while authorship of suggestions will not be shared publically, library worker evaluations and, in general, worker opinion are also useful information for managers and supervisors to use for judging the organization's success in meeting its customer service goals.

All this number crunching takes planning and a lot of time and effort. In a large library system, for example, data may flow in from dozens of branches or in digital format, while in a small but busy in-person environment, hundreds of comments may flow in. Most information is typically in the form of written comments from the public. What preplanning is needed? Whose job will it be to collate this information into a usable format for all staff to look at? How will sources of data from several disparate sources be combined to give a full picture of library operations? How much of this data will need to be rekeyed or entered into spreadsheets? It may indeed seem like a great deal of work, but without effective feedback, management's best efforts to promote a customer service program may fade because library workers will never know how they are doing. They will never get to check their "score" with the public (more on this later). In addition, without including comments and responses, workers may feel as if they do not have enough opportunities to assess a customer service program or customer service performance.

Ongoing assessment is important as well. Continuous customer service training requires a continuous flow of data. Management can help to both relieve the burdens of information overload and of constant reporting by allowing staff the time to digest information and take advantage of training opportunities.

In this chapter, we will address ways to collect data (especially from customers) as well as methods for assessing worker responses to customer service programs, and how this customer service feedback can be used to pedagogically effective ends.

Many elements of customer service programs in organizations are grounded in a variety of theories. These theories can include communication theories for identifying styles and approaches to customers, marketing theories for identifying customer needs and wants, and research theories for assessing data gathered. One theory directly related to customer service program elements is the Gap Theory of Assessment. How does this theory relate to customer service and successful assessment of customer service?

Using the Gap Theory of Assessment

The Gap Theory is specifically an assessment theory. The theory, considered an assessment tool, is a little over two decades old and is grounded in the Gap Theory of Service Quality. This tool is a for-profit process created by a marketing research group (Parasuraman, Zeithaml and Berry) and was considered the result of ground-breaking research known as SERVQUAL—designed to measure service quality across five dimensions: reliability, assurance, tangibles, empathy, and responsiveness. This is done through questions asked of random samples of customers from three perspectives (perceived, desired, and minimum) using Likert scales, typically one through nine. Those gaps identified in assessing data were then used to determine the service issues needing attention. Librarianship's interpretation of SERVQUAL is LIBQUAL+. Following the identification of gaps in service, a customer service program is designed to address needs. Random samples are then again conducted, after identified periods of service implementation, and compared to original survey data to re-identify customer perspectives and determine if gaps have been filled or needs have been met.

Surveying Methods of Collecting Customer Feedback

A variety of options exist to collect customer response. Each has its own characteristics and purposes, and each will create differing training needs.

Response Cards

Response cards can be either completed on-site at point-of-use or returned by mail, fax, or in person. Many organizations and businesses simply display stacks of response cards or mailers, while others actively solicit responses. Response cards offer the ability to gather data from a large number of customers at all times or specific times.

Training issues: As with any other method of feedback, workers should receive information on why the data is being collected and the collection outcomes. Staff and volunteers who agree with the need for feedback will be more willing to actively solicit customers to complete the data-collecting forms. Libraries should train workers to call attention to the feedback process and card and handle response cards discretely. Curiosity is a human desire, and reading the cards will provide immediate feedback, but any perusal of response cards collected should be performed out of view of the customers. Library workers should be trained in the sequence for collecting the forms and forwarding them to a supervisor. Also, staff and volunteers should be trained to know when a customer complaint is serious or extensive enough to warrant more than a customer response card. Some response card processes include locked response boxes with access only by administration, and in organizations located in cities, counties, or other types of environments that are involved in extensive customer service assessment processes, sealed response-card boxes are returned not to library administration first but to umbrella-organization administration.

All customer training information recommends measurement and evaluation of general aspects of the customer service program as well as its specific elements, including customer and employee interactions, signage, and environment. Evaluation can take many forms; however, most training programs recommend providing a response mechanism for customers. In today's world that response includes:

Printed "In-person" Cards

- Available to be picked up (placed throughout the library for random completion)
- Handed out at specific intervals (during evaluation week, on the busiest days)
- Handed out continuously (every book checked out contains a response card)
- Handed out in specific situations (when a worker and customer have a negative interaction, a service cannot be completed, a resource is unavailable, a class is completed)

Online Response Cards

- Available for response (on library Web site in a variety of places for random completion)
- Sent at specific intervals (e-mail requests to assess during evaluation week or during a high online request time; pop-up after site use or library worker/customer interaction)
- Sent out continuously (every online interaction has a request for response e-mailed out)
- Sent out at specific situations (when a library worker and customer have a negative interaction, a service cannot be completed, a resource is unavailable, an online tutorial is completed)

Eye-catching Response Systems

Trendy, clever, and unique responses can be eye-catching in themselves or can be asked at unusual times to attract attention—and they can be aggregate or individualized).

- Posted butcher paper with comment pens for responses during an unveiling of a new environment, service, or resource or during a construction or renovation
- Blogs (allowing customer postings) established to gather feedback for existing or new services or resources
- Containers with, for example, marbles to move from a "loved it" jar to a "needs work" jar for quick assessment by youth customers
- A phone-answering mechanism designed to take phone responses on customer services

Why cover these important elements in a book about training for customer service? When response mechanisms are used it is important for managers to carefully choose and construct the information gathered. Although we should make measurement valid and not handicap library workers with information that is lengthy to assess, it is even more important to choose questions—when the response is not just a general, open-ended "Tell us how we're doing!" approach—that match customer service program goals and training content. For example:

Instead of...	*Use...*
Comments on your inter-actions with employees?	Did library workers greet you when you approached the public service desks? (Use when training includes greeting scripts and requirements for greeting.)
	Did library workers ask you if you received the resources you needed? (Use when program and training include requirements for using probing closure statements.)
Does the library signage meet your needs?	Do library signs clearly illustrate service areas for your use, such as "check out" and "information?" (Use when the customer service program provides new signs that use fewer "library" words such as *circulation* and/or *reference*.)

Because response mechanisms are an important part of evaluating the customer service program, they should:

- Be assessed to make sure that adequate time is given to employees for their application of customer service curriculum
- Avoid offering only an open-ended approach to answering questions so that questions can assess specific program training goals

Surveys

Everyone loves surveys—until they have to do them. As anyone who has ever conducted a survey knows, it is a particularly challenging way to gather information. Good survey questions are hard to write, and collecting responses is labor-intensive, to say nothing of inputting (for print surveys) and analyzing the data afterward. But for evaluating customer service, nothing is more effective than directly, personally asking customers, in some way, their opinion of the service they just received. This is so for several reasons, including the certainty and immediacy of the reaction (how many times have you taken a response card with the best of intentions of returning it?), the ability to record longer answers, the specificity of the interaction and the assessment, and the opportunity to ask follow-up questions.

Training issues: Workers who are going to conduct the surveys, whether by phone or in person, need to be trained in survey methodology, including how to greet and approach customers, how to ask specific assessment questions and then follow-up questions, how to get quiet respondents to say more, and how to get talkative respondents to wrap it up. Management should explain the importance of collecting the information and have a plan to share the information gathered in these surveys with all workers in public and support service areas.

(In all data collection, remember the importance of sharing the data with the individuals who were asked to collect it.)

Suggestion Boxes

Libraries, as do many organizations, have suggestion boxes to collect customer comments. Virtual suggestion boxes are also common on Web sites. Suggestion boxes invite comments, both signed and anonymous, that presumably make respondents more willing to be honest in their appraisals.

Training issues: Library workers should encourage the public when appropriate to submit their comments. Comment cards with specific questions may get more specific (that is, useful) responses than blank cards. Also, blank cards invite offensive, suggestive, or insulting comments, sometimes directed at individuals. Suggestion box comments should be responded to, especially when customers request a response. Recurring questions, which can be answered individually or grouped together for aggregate response, deserve a public posting, either in a posting area in the library or on the Web page. Library workers should be clear on who should respond to suggestion box comments and, if they are delegated the responsibility to respond, they should have parameters for responding. Finally, a decision should be made up front as to who receives the postings from online suggestion boxes and what parameters they have in responding.

Clipboards and Other Public Methods

Some libraries have experimented with methods of soliciting comments that involve having customers add comments to various forms of public forums. In an online environment, this might take the form of public comments posted to a Web site or blog. In the physical world, this can be accomplished with a clipboard stationed in a public area, a suggestion board, posted butcher paper, or other device located where everyone can read everyone else's comments. The advantage is that threads can develop where one respondent notes what other respondents have written and adds to it. The disadvantage is that some customers might be intimidated into not being totally honest in their responses. Another obvious disadvantage is inappropriate language or images being posted publicly.

Training issues: Staff and employees should be trained to encourage customers to add their comments, but they should not rush over after every comment and look at the board. There will be time to get the comments later. Also, staff and volunteers will need to understand when a complaint or other comment is appropriate for the clipboard or Web log and when it is not. If a customer is concerned about a policy and wants a response from administration, workers should be trained to make every attempt to handle the situation but also offer a complaint form. Library workers will also need to know that some comments, such as complaints naming specific staff and obscene or profane suggestions and comments, should not remain in the public view and should be given techniques to excise inappropriate information without compromising other data. Other than that, staff and volunteers should let the discussion lead where it will.

Complaint Forms

The complaint form is one type of customer feedback device that many libraries probably already have in place. And staff and volunteers are most likely already trained in how to use it. Complaint forms (though they may go by a variety of euphemistic names, such as accident reports) are necessary for those situations when the customer wants to challenge a library policy or procedure and that concern must be routed up the chain of command. The customer, who may or may not wish to include his or her name, still wants the complaint to be registered and considered. Typically, libraries will and should have separate forms for materials challenges—especially if the process of handling them is different from other policies—or sometimes the form may be the same.

Training issues: On a procedural basis, staff and volunteers will need to know when the complaint form is appropriate and where to route it. On the more important and difficult level of interpersonal communications, workers will need to know what to say to the customer who is complaining, how to take the complaint, and how to discuss the customer's concern. In many organizations, the complaint form is seen as a buffer to diffuse the complaint, provide a channel for the complaint, and to furnish a way to manage the complaint so that it does not end up on the desk of a city councilman or college dean or in the media. If this is the case, workers need to understand this and the importance of handling the customer's interaction in offering and receiving the complaint form. Although an obvious statement would be that workers need training in completing forms, this is a critical part of the process. Forms need to be completed and handled consistently with times, names or initials of staff that have participated and handled the situation, and techniques for the language (neutral, specific) used to complete forms.

Mystery Shoppers

Although mystery shoppers are not technically customers but rather individuals posing as customers, they are used as a way to see the organization from the perspective of customers. When used appropriately and judiciously, mystery shoppers can provide valuable information about customer service in the organization.

Training issues: Since by design, the mystery shoppers will be unknown to the library staff, they cannot anticipate a specific response. The training implications will be felt when providing the feedback. Management may want to announce that mystery shoppers will be used in the annual customer service program and why and how the information they collect will be used, but not when the window for mystery shoppers might or will appear. Resentment regarding the technique will be mitigated if employees are told, in general, that mystery shoppers are part of the annual assessment process and if they understand that the goal is to improve service and not to punish. Any verbal or written reports should be shared with the managers of those facilities only. General and aggregate comments on service throughout the organization should be shared with everyone and used as a basis for training in targeted areas. Egregious behavior specific to individuals or departments or groups should be shared in the formal discipline or evaluation process.

Focus Groups

Focus groups provide a different kind of customer feedback regarding the development of library service in general as well as specific or targeted services. Focus groups may include regular users as well those who do not use the library. Users, of course, can relay information about needed services and how to improve existing services. Nonusers will be able to provide insight about why they do not use the library and what it would take to make them library users. Focus groups can be used for assessing resources, facilities, and customer service and are also often turned to the development of services in a new location or as a way of establishing the need for a new program or service. They are thought to be excellent ways of getting a quick response to questions and common impressions. When groups are well organized and managed, they are an efficient and effective way of gathering a range and depth of feedback in a short period of time. Another obvious fact about focus groups is that they can be used as a marketing tool for communicating information about the library, its services, and its resources to both general and targeted groups of users and nonusers. Obvious challenges to focus groups include: it is often hard to analyze responses; skill in facilitating is critical to success; and getting groups together may be difficult.

Training issues: Conducting focus groups requires planning, scripts for questions and process and some basic training. (See Resource Tool E: "Using Focus Groups in Assessing Customer Service.") Participants should be encouraged to speak uninterrupted, or if unresponsive, they should be prompted to speak. Staff and volunteers should be advised to note comments without responding, to avoid the appearance of being defensive. Some workers of the branch or unit involved should be present at the focus group meetings to hear and assimilate the comments firsthand. And the organization should, collectively, be ready to implement the results of the focus group or, if not feasible, at least seriously consider the responses in the customer service program assessment content.

Observation

Observing employee and customer interactions is sometimes used to assess an organization's customer service program. Observation might be used to gather specific, accurate information about how scripts are being used, how interactions such as greetings and closures are occurring, how processes might be followed, and how conflicts are being handled. It is clear that observation provides "real time" views of operations and interactions as they are occurring. Using observation as a customer service assessment offers challenges as well, and these include possible difficulties in interpreting behaviors; difficulties in recording, grouping, or categorizing specific actions and activities; the expense of identifying, training, and hiring workers to carry out these observations; and the strong possibility that observers will influence the behavior of employees and even customers because they are aware they are being observed.

Training issues: Workers able to observe need a variety of competencies and training. The latter includes training in recognizing and grouping behaviors and in completing forms. Training issues related to using observation include:

- The better, more consistent observations occur when fewer individuals work more hours and shifts, as opposed to a wider variety of people working a few hours at a time (for consistency in interpretation and form completion).
- Staff and volunteers need training in ignoring observers and the observation process.

Interviews

A little used, expensive, and time-consuming technique for gathering assessment is interviewing. Interviewing is an expanded, targeted approach to identifying customers who have been served and requesting an in-depth interview for assessing their levels of satisfaction with the customer service they received. Interview techniques can be used in several ways:

- Individuals who have responded to customer service questionnaires are interviewed post questionnaire completion for clarification and/or expanded information.
- Individuals who have completed customer service interactions are asked for an in-depth interview to assess services received.
- Individuals identified following focus group participations are asked for an in-depth interview.

Interviews can provide managers with a wealth of information, and this attention to customers and assessing their perceptions and interactions can assist organizations in building customer relationships.

Training issues: Interviewers need in-depth interviewing skills and often need more extensive information about the organization.

The challenges of interviewing include the expertise needed by the interviewers, the training needed, the possibly extensive cost, the amount of post-interview time needed for transcription and analysis, and the difficulty in analyzing and comparing data among interviewer content.

Evaluating Volunteer Customer Service

Materials recommending volunteer guidebooks and manuals always mention the recommendation for including volunteers in a performance evaluating process. This process—although it may not be exactly like the employee's process—sends the message that the volunteers work is a critical part of the workplace. It also gives staff and the volunteer coordinator the ability to equitably manage volunteers, providing recommendations for volunteers to receive training to enhance their work, to change jobs, or send to realize that the library might not be the best match for his or her interests and abilities. Volunteer evaluation forms need to have questions that speak to:

- general customer service—if volunteer job responsibilities—including external customer service work,
- internal customer service—for all volunteers,
- a commitment to both the initial and ongoing training needed to complete volunteer tasks,
- a knowledge of and commitment to the vision, mission, and goals of the organization in general and as they relate to the organization's customers.

Utilizing Feedback in Training

Now that you have collected—by the various means outlined above—a good amount of customer feedback, what do you do with it? How do you process that data in such a way that it will improve service in your organization? In short, how do you listen to what your customers are telling you?

The most important rule is that you have to take what they are saying seriously. Staff at all levels must be trained to pay attention to the comments. This involves both helping the customer to overcome the natural resistance to asking a question and then how to train staff to see the customer's comment not as a threat but an opportunity. Once this has occurred, it is a short jump to training staff not only to be receptive to comments that arise, but even proactive in asking for comment. We can all be trained to see customer response as our "score"—telling us how we are doing and providing us with opportunities to improve our performance.

Management can foster this change in attitude by making sure that assessment data and comments that are collected find their way back. There are several ways to do this, starting with sharing comments. They should be shared first with the management team and other administrators, then any customer service committee or team, and then throughout the organization. All library workers should know exactly how to access this data and be encouraged to refer to it as a way of checking on their progress. Management can and should share the raw response data, but the more thoughtful and effective method will involve using the data to plan targeted training to improve performance. Later in this chapter, we will provide greater detail about how to both share data and incorporate it into training, but before exploring those topics, we need to consider an important training issue, specifically, the art of taking a complaint.

Teaching Staff and Volunteers to Take Complaints

Everyone dreads a complaint. Perhaps it is because no one likes conflict. Perhaps it is because we do not want to believe that someone would not like the job that we do. And certainly, the fact that some customers seem to relish being very harsh, and often personal, in their complaints does not help matters. But complaints are a normal and unavoidable aspect of public service. Anyone who has worked with the public knows that sooner or later someone will complain. Contrary to seeing the complaint as a negative, however, staff at all levels and volunteers can be taught to view the complaint as a moment of opportunity in serving the public. A complaint is an opportunity because it represents a moment when a member of the public is disturbed about the service they received in the library. If the complaint is handled poorly, it will confirm the customer's poor opinion of the entire organization. This customer will leave, possibly never to return, but also likely to tell others of the shabby treatment received at the library. If, however, the complaint is handled well, if the customer can leave feeling that his or her complaint was handled thoughtfully and respectfully, then she or he will become a convert to the organization, a believer who will tell friends about the wonderful service received at the library. Note that we do not say that customers have to get what they want, only *that the complaint is handled well*. While it certainly helps the outcome if you can give them whatever they want, it is often not possible and not even necessary to be perceived as offering good customer service. In most situations, there are ways to say no and to hold your ground that will create a favorable outcome and turn the complainer into a believer. In addition, the reality is that a fair number of customer service complaints come from customers who do not get the book they need or cannot get on a computer or cannot stay past their allotted time on the computer. Therefore, actively working with customers—rather than just getting them what they want—or the customer service response to the interaction is critical.

How does this favorable outcome occur? With training, common sense, and a positive attitude. Staff must see the complaint as an opportunity rather than a threat. This is difficult, but it has been accomplished in many organizations. The key is to give the staff tools to respond to complaints. The more they are in control of the situation, the more comfortable they will feel, which, in turn, will equip them to confidently see the complaint as a potential opportunity.

So what do you teach library workers to do in responding to complaints? Here are a few suggestions:

Avoid taking comments personally or being defensive. Although not all complaints include personal observations, comments, or issues, staff and volunteers should be trained in how not to take comments personally whether based on perception or on words, tone or voice, or whether nonverbal language is used. Defensiveness is resistance. The words that are playing through a defensive library worker's mind are something like this: *No! That's not right. We offer great service here. We would never do a thing like that. I know our staff or volunteers would never treat a member of the public rudely.* Complaints are about the service that the customer received. You can train your staff to say to themselves, as the people are complaining, *This is not about you; this is about the library. These people seem upset. I need to acknowledge their concern, then find ways to make them feel better about the library and their visit.* Remind everyone that complaints are opportunities not threats.

Withhold judgment. Avoid the tendency to believe that just because customers are complaining about your service, they are wrong. They may turn out to have a valid point of view. Who knows, you might even agree with their point of view (though, of course, it does not matter whether you agree with them.) But whether you agree or not, understand that the people speaking to you are troubled and your job is to hear them out and to describe to the complainers what your process will be in meeting their concerns.

Listen. Let the customers talk. This does two things: it buys you time to think, and it allows them to work off steam. You may find that often just having someone hear them out is all they want. Once they have been allowed to state their concerns, you can often reason with them more calmly and logically. You may even find that they are content to merely lodge the complaint without requiring any further action.

Use positive language. You can teach staff techniques for handling a complaint in ways that allow them to maintain control over the situation. In Chapter 1, we discussed specific phrases that you can give your staff to help them diffuse the situation. These positive, soothing scripted phrases are designed to signal to customers that you are hearing their complaint while calming their nerves.

Scripts

The use of positive language brings us to a discussion of scripts. As we have commented at several points in this book, scripts provide an excellent way to give library workers the language that will empower them to respond effectively to the public. The positive phrases spoken of above are critical, but sometimes management may find it necessary to write out the entire conversation with a member of the public, to have the staff study the script, and to be prepared to work from the script. These scripts can predict the kind of conversations that are likely to arise and will provide staff the tools for taking part in them.

Consider for a moment the exchange presented in Figure 5.1. Each of the phrases used by James in this conversation can be used to counter these very standard comments. Note that James never became defensive but answered each question or comment with a positive response that acknowledged the customer's concern and then offered solutions. In this sample conversation, as is often the case in actual exchanges, James managed to turn a disgruntled customer into a happy customer and ensured that he will return again and again. Also note the subtle way that he trained the customer: James informed him of the existence of a service—being able to place a hold on a book—that the customer will use again in the future and that will make use of the library easier and more enjoyable for the customer (and the staff, too).

Role-playing in a Group Setting

Another way to train staff to listen for comments and to be responsive is to act out exchanges with customers in a group setting. This will work well for meetings or in staff-development day programs. Give one library worker the role of the customer and another the role of staff member or volunteer. Let them play

Figure 5.1 **Sample Script: Positive Responses**	
James the circulation supervisor	Did you find everything you need, Sir?
Customer	Actually, no. In fact, I seldom find what I need here.
James	I'm sorry to hear that. Is there anything I can help you find?
Customer	I was looking for that new bestseller about George Washington.
James	Yes, we do have that book, but unfortunately, all our copies are checked out. I would be happy to put your name on the list. The wait shouldn't be too long.
Customer	Oh. Okay. I never thought of that. You'll call me when it comes in and everything?
James	Absolutely.
Customer	Okay then, I will. But you people need to get more copies of the bestsellers.
James	I will make a note of your comment and let our branch manager know.
Customer	Thanks. You know, you've been very helpful.
James	Thank you. Is there anything else I can help you find?

out scenarios that illustrate how to listen for and respond to complaints. As the staff practice how to listen for comments, ask for feedback, take complaints, and administer surveys or other information gathering, they will grow more proficient in an environment where they are not being watched (and judged) by the public. In good role-playing exercises, staff and volunteers will have fun and get into their roles. Encourage them to have a good time and indulge in good-natured critiques of one another's role-playing. Be sure to have managers participate in role-playing exercises because they need the training and because workers need to see that they take responsibility for their part in serving the public.

Another method for role-playing is to stage a series of skits that show first how not to handle certain customer service interactions, followed immediately with skits showing the right way. The how-not-to-do-it skits will inevitably draw great howls of laughter not only because the skits will be over-the-top funny in showing all the wrong things to do, but also because staff will recognize their coworkers in the skits and will be happy to see that others have recognized that type of problem. Following the how-not-to skits, the staff can call out their comments about how the behavior went wrong and how it could be improved.

Whether you ask individuals to create their own role-playing on the spot or stage a series of instructive skits, you can use the feedback from your customers to focus the point of your program. The data you collect from your customers will help you to shape training in exactly the areas that matter to your customers.

Sharing Customer Feedback with Staff

As we have stated previously in this chapter, one of the most critical keys to developing buy-in to the goals and outcomes of customer service is to share customer feedback. Call it competitive, call it evaluative, but all people want to know how they are doing. Everyone wants to know his or her score. We each carry with us a set of evaluations that are important to us: our golf score, the number of comic books in our collection, our weight since starting the new diet, the number of years we have been married, our annual salary. For each person the score is different, but we all measure our accomplishments against a score.

In our work life it is no different; we want to know how we are doing. And management wants to know too. If our objective is to please the customers (more a bit later in this chapter on why we want to please the customers), we want to know if they were pleased. There are direct and indirect indications of whether they were pleased. The indirect indications are that they return, that they check out a lot of books, that they come through the turnstile in ever-increasing numbers, that they attend programs in flocks. The direct indications are that they find what they need at the library and, in an outcomes mode, that their lives change in positive ways because of what they found at the library. We are happy to know if they are satisfied with the library, but what we really want to know is if they got a job because of the resume books they checked out, that they passed their citizenship test because of the ESL classes that were offered, that they did better in first grade because they were exposed to books in preschool story hours. We will know these things only if we ask them, so we have to ask them. And as we discussed above, we will ask them many other things as well that are not as outcomes oriented: Did we have what you needed? Were our library workers helpful? What do you like best about the library? What could we do better?

When we have collected all this data, and after management has taken a first pass, the data must then be shared. This is important for several reasons. First, as we have said before, workers need to get their score; they need to know how they are doing. Only then will they know whether any of their efforts at customer service are paying off. Only then will they know what they have to improve. Second, if management wants library workers to reorient their objectives toward outcomes, their work needs to be measured against outcomes and their score needs to be given back to them in terms of the outcomes—not just the number of books circulated—although output data of this sort has its place— but also the percentage of customers who found the book or subject matter they were looking for. Third, their score gives a numerical reference, a benchmark, against which to measure progress both against their earlier performance and against the performance of other units (branches, departments, and so forth).

Methods of Sharing Customer Feedback and Service Data

So how do you share data? Obviously, numerical data is easier to share than narrative data (for example, comments in a suggestion box or on a clipboard), but on some level of detail, all data can be shared. Here are some suggestions:

- *Post numerical data where all library workers can access it.* This is most readily done by posting it to a Web site, but the data can also be e-mailed to all workers or to managers to be shared with workers. All numerical data should be shared, including service data from the library's circulation system, as well as evaluation data, survey results, and so forth.

- Create binders of written comments available for all to review.
- Prepare digests of comments to illustrate common themes.
- Review customer feedback data in staff and volunteer meetings.
- Incorporate customer feedback in training programs.

Before you go and share the data, however, it should be noted that there are some ground rules to distributing the data. Here are the dos and don'ts:

- *Return data to the level at which it was collected.* Data collected from all departments and branches can be collated and shared with all units of the system. Conversely, data that pertains to only a specific unit should be shared with only that unit on a regular basis.
- *Strip negative personal comments and attacks from narrative data.* While feedback pertaining to specific library workers should be passed along to those individuals, negative comments of that sort should be viewed in the context of personnel information that is always confidential. Sharing compliments about specific employees is another matter—public praise is always welcome.
- *If you post numerical data to a Web page, keep it current.* If you are going to go to the trouble to post the information, make sure it stays current. There is nothing worse than posting data for a period of time, getting everyone used to measuring their performance by those data, then pulling it. Similarly, if you have done only one survey, there is little training value to posting that data at all—distributing the results will be preferable.
- *If you post numerical data, do not constantly change the categories.* Find the measures that you feel most directly tell the story and keep those data current. Changing the categories sends a message that management intentions are ambiguous, and staff and volunteers will lose interest.
- *Focus on a few key indicators of success and count those.* In other words, do not try to count everything.
- *Allow enough historical data to accumulate to make a meaningful comparison.* Comparison data will be most instructive over the long haul. Only then will trends emerge.

Summarizing Customer Feedback Strategies

What is the ultimate goal of customer service? In the private sector it is to make money and increase the business by building clientele. In the public and nonprofit sectors, it is to ensure the long-term viability of the institution. How is that accomplished? In the public sector, as in the private sector, the solution lies in creating the all-important return customer. The return customer not only comes back again and again but also tells friends and family about the service. The customer returns when she finds the experience of visiting the library to be worth her time. The customer finds the experience worth her time when she finds the visit productive and pleasurable. The customer needs to find what she came for and she needs to encounter helpful and efficient employees.

Is this the basis you use to evaluate your staff and volunteers when it comes to customer service? It is a simple equation, but it is easy to get sidetracked onto less significant concerns: Did the employee always remember to smile? Did she stick to the script? Did she forget to wear her nametag? These might be real indicators of the individual's attention or lack thereof to customer service needs, but the goal of the entire organization should be to ensure that the customer's visit to the library is productive and pleasurable and that he or she is going to become a return customer. Each library worker has a role to play in that equation, from the page that gets the books back on the shelf quickly and in the right place to the circulation clerk who pleasantly and accurately manages the customer's accounts to the reference librarian who explores all options to fill requests.

Library worker evaluation is a form of training that allows the supervisor to instruct workers in customer service priorities. At an evaluation, a staff member or volunteer can learn the ways in which she or he is effectively, or not effectively, serving the public. The thoughtful evaluation will provide guidance from the supervisor to the library worker in how to help ensure that library users will return. The evaluation gives an opportunity for the supervisor to stress the key elements of customer service as defined by the organization. In each annual evaluation, the supervisor should tell staff and volunteers exactly what performance is expected in all aspects of the work, and customer service should always be included. Each library worker should leave the evaluation interview with a clear idea of what is expected.

You may work in a situation where your parent organization requires a standard performance evaluation form. This form may or may not address customer service as one of its criteria, or, if it does, it may not address the specific aspects of service that you find most critical in your library. If not, you may have one of several options. First, find out if you can change the form to add customer service elements. Your human resources department will probably not allow this because the point of a standard form is to hold all employees to a common standard. The human resources department may, however, be able to use a supplemental form that specifically addresses customer service. It may also be possible—perhaps even recommended—to provide employees with a narrative evaluation. This narrative should explain to employees in which areas they have done well, which ones they need to work on. The employees should be asked to note what training they need to do their job better, and that training component should be noted in the employees' evaluation. In larger systems, this information can be collated across departments and sites to provide a training plan for library staff that will leverage training budgets to achieve real improvements in customer service.

6

Planning Staff-Development Days

Staff-development days represent one of many opportunities to incorporate all facets of customer service learning into the library's training plans. Because many libraries invest a great deal of time and effort into these events—which frequently also involve the service impact of closing the library for a day—we will spend this chapter exploring ways to approach staff days (for all library workers) that will provide the greatest amount of return on the investment for management, staff, and volunteers.

For some time, libraries have been investing in staff days for training. Investing in this critical training time includes the planning, design, and delivery of the event or activity—all "at cost" to the library budget. The issues surrounding staff days, however, are many and include not only the budget or cost issues but also concerns for how staff days are to be used for training and education and, for many, most important, permissions for library facilities to be closed to customers for the entire day. While enthusiasm for staff days has waxed and waned owing to these issues, personnel in public schools and higher education have typically been required to attend training provided by the institution. Often called "in-service" training, these activities have provided a relatively low-cost way for K–12 and higher education faculty and staff to learn about changes to policies and procedures, brush up old skills, update their knowledge of emerging practices in their fields, and create a team kickoff for new semesters and academic years.

In public libraries, the idea has come and gone, often because of cost issues and very often owing to concerns related to closing to the public for any length of time. In fact, it has not been uncommon for city, county, and board leadership to greatly affect whether support for this half day or full day of training has been forthcoming. Oddly enough, cuts in training and staff-development budgets—specifically when travel funds are cut—have allowed many library environments to make an excellent case for a lower cost, more effective way—staff full or half days—to get all employees on the same page. In addition, public umbrella organizations committed to integrated, continuous learning from the older Total Quality Management (TQM) philosophy, have returned to supporting staff day activities, since they provide the venue for discussing the commitment to the vision and policies and procedures associated with a pervasive approach to customer service.

This approach to training and education has been found by administrators to be an excellent technique to build camaraderie while providing training across all levels of management, staff, and volunteers. For all types of libraries, and especially those with multiple outlets, staff days will also allow all library workers to meet their coworkers from other sites, thus providing opportunities to train across facilities, trade ideas, and develop a feeling of team spirit. One of the real benefits from these days, however, is in the design and delivery of training within this specific half-day or whole-day venue. Staff days provide the mechanism for delivering a *consistent* message with the same content to all employees and workers in the same environment, with the same examples and impromptu discussion, and at the same time. This uniformity of delivery offers management an excellent opportunity to bring all library workers onto the same page by means of clearly established expectations, a tight timeline for practice and beginning delivery, and the universal parameters for enhanced opportunities for assessment. For these reasons, the topic of customer service is one of the best possible subject areas to explore on staff-development days.

Not surprisingly, many libraries spend much time preparing for staff day, including decorating the library and conducting theme-related activities during the day. When the Piscataway (N.J.) Public Library trained its staff in the Fish!® Customer Service Model, Director Anne Roman and her staff used fish-related decorations throughout the library. Austin Community College staff-day themes over the years have incorporated decorations, advertising, handouts, and icebreakers along theme lines that have included a getaway island theme, complete with shiny collapsible palm trees and passports; a mystery theme with detective badges; and a movie-going theme with training in management centered around the movie "Twelve O'Clock High" that included popcorn, hotdogs, movie tickets, and a guess-the-movie-star icebreaker. The Riverside County Library System has held an annual staff day since 2000 that involves a six-month planning effort by a committee of staff members. (See the case study in this chapter for more information on how this library system introduced a major customer service initiative in the context of staff-development day.)

Launching a First Event

Holding an effective staff-development day requires a good amount of planning and organization. Before embarking on presenting a staff day, you should probably consider the following:

- *Budget.* You can think of a staff-development day as a miniconference, and successful conferences require resources. There are ways to cut corners and economize and produce an effective event without spending huge amounts of money; however, you will need to have some budget for the event. In planning your day, consider the amount of money you have to spend for speakers, meals, and special activities to determine how elaborate your event will be. Do not forget that time is money as well. Most organizations do not have staff whose job responsibilities are devoted year-round to staff development, so those hours spent planning, picking up, and so forth are typically spent providing other services.

- *Staff resources.* What expertise do your library workers have to prepare for and present your staff day? Using a staff committee to prepare for the event is highly recommended because of the many details necessary for pulling off a successful event and to ensure buy-in from staff in the event. In preparation, consider drawing on staff and volunteers who are creative, energetic, and upbeat. In picking your presenters, allow staff who are willing to rise to the occasion to share their expertise with their colleagues. However, forcing those to present who are not willing or allowing staff to present who are not suitable will undermine your event. And also keep in mind that a staff member who is presenting is not in a session learning.

- *Closing the library.* To be most successful, all staff must be allowed—in fact, required—to attend the staff-development day, and volunteers should be invited to attend. This is particularly important when introducing customer service topics that affect every library worker. To do this, you will have to close your library for the day. Reasonable governing boards and the public will usually understand and approve of closing the library for an annual event that will have a positive impact on library, but if you cannot get that approval, you will have to consider an alternative to a staff-development day.

- *What are your goals?* As you begin to plan your staff development day, you should give some thought to your goals for the event. Do you intend to use the day as a way to introduce a bold new initiative, to strengthen staff skills, to build team spirit, to reinforce policy and procedure, or for more than one of these reasons? Clarifying your goals in terms of strategic outcomes will help you to decide how to steer staff in their planning of the event. In planning a first staff-day event, you may wish to have relatively modest goals and allow staff to get used to the idea of staff-development day, which, in itself, represents an element of change in their environment. Launching significant changes on your first staff day may establish expectations or even apprehensions about future staff days.

- *One-time or recurring?* You may find it wise not to tout your staff day as a "first annual" staff day if you are not absolutely sure you will have the resources and support to hold staff day again next year. It is likely that most staff will very much enjoy the day and, like other library managers, you will find it an effective way to provide information and training for all library workers. However, do not be discouraged if you cannot hold a staff-development day every year. You may opt for a staff-day event scheduled every other year or irregularly. Remember, a well-planned event is what is important, so make the most of your time and do not worry about frequency.

Making Staff Day Effective

Assuming that you have considered the foregoing questions and have decided to hold a staff day, you can now proceed to the following set of considerations for making the day effective:

- *Who will be the planning team?* Picking your planning team will be your first challenge. As stated above, creativity and positive attitude are the most important qualities in a planning team member. They should see the reason for the staff day and share your vision for how it can benefit library staff and customers. This is especially important if you are presenting customer service topics; negativity on the planning committee will derail your best-laid plans. Try to pick staff from various levels and departments in the library, including children's, adult services, and circulation staff, and if your library has a large number of volunteers consider having volunteers as part of the planning team. Avoid having only the management team plan the event. And in subsequent years, rotate members off the committee to allow more staff to participate in planing the event. This will keep new ideas coming and allow staff to appreciate the amount of work that goes into planning the day.
- *Who will be your presenters?* Are you going to use staff as presenters, or seek outside presenters? This will depend on what messages you want to deliver, what talent is available on staff, and what you have to spend for presenters. If you have no budget for presenters, you will have to consider using staff and/or volunteers (including being a presenter yourself), calling on staff of neighboring libraries, or asking local individuals with expertise to help present. You may be able to bring in outside speakers who will waive a fee but for whom you will need to pay travel expenses. Look to cooperative library systems, the state library, your state association, or other library groups for speakers. Vendors of services to libraries also may be willing to send staff to help with presentations. As you evaluate your event after the fact, pay attention to how library workers respond to internal versus external speakers. Sometimes staff will find a message coming from an external speaker carries more authority than one from a fellow staff member, but this will probably depend on the specific subject. Generally speaking, a mix of internal and external speakers will probably be most desirable.
- *Will you use a "canned" curriculum or do it yourself?* In planning a customer service presentation for your staff day, you will have to decide if you are going to use one of the several products that exist on the market or develop your own initiative. If you have limited staff resources, but you

do have money to spend, renting a film or hiring a presenter will probably be preferable. On the other hand, you may want to invest the time and energy in creating an initiative that belongs to just your library. This will ultimately create more buy-in from library workers than would a model imposed by another organization and may be especially useful if you want your customer service model to be integrated into your overall management philosophy (see Riverside County Library System case history at the end of this section). Either way, the approach you choose should be done so with consideration of your ultimate customer service strategy for your library.

- *What will your format be?* A wide variety of choices in format exists. You can use group sessions, breakouts, concurrent sessions, structured and unstructured interactions, and other formats. Your choice of formats will be influenced by the facility you use, the size of your staff, the number of presenters available to you, and the content of your presentations. Messages that you want the entire staff to hear will have to be delivered in plenary sessions, while specialized information will need to be delivered in concurrent or breakout sessions.

- *How will you handle food?* Anyone who has ever put on a meeting will not be surprised to learn that food can make or break a meeting experience. If you gather staff together for a daylong training, feeding them will have several benefits: you will avoid the downtime necessary for going to get food, keep the group together and preserve momentum, solve their basic human needs so that they can concentrate on learning, and give your staff something nice that will make them look forward to the event again next year. It is not necessary to spend a fortune on food, but be sure that you have a reliable caterer that will produce good-tasting food on time. Other food issues include having food for special-needs staff, making sure that healthy food is available, and providing food that is available throughout the day instead of just at meal or even break times.

- *Share your goals for the day with everyone.* Let everyone, including your umbrella administration, know the goals you have for the day. Invite administrators, board members, and Friends to be introduced and to attend sessions of interest.

- *How will you evaluate success?* You will likely want to evaluate how you have succeeded in meeting your strategic goals for the day while providing a rewarding and worthwhile experience for your staff and volunteers. The only way to know if staff found it rewarding is to ask. Evaluation forms should offer the opportunity to rate the day not in terms of whether it was liked or not, as well as whether they feel the content was helpful and relevant to them personally, especially to how they do their jobs. Be sure to ask all attendees to rate both the entire day as well as individual sessions. Also, provide attendees an opportunity to give you ideas for next year's staff day. Additional areas to assess include: how library customers "handled" the library being closed for the day or, if alternative services were provided, how customers responded to these services. This assessment is especially critical

---

Figure 6-1
Case Study: Introducing STARS Service at the Riverside County Library System
Staff-Development Day

During fall 2004 and spring 2005, the management team of the Riverside County Library System (RCLS) determined that the time had arrived to make customer service a central element of library management. The management team wanted to develop a comprehensive approach to customer service that ranged from changing behavior in customer interactions to providing a framework for training to a new system of communications within the organization to systematic methods for soliciting customer feedback. Much time and discussion was devoted to a consideration of how to ensure buy-in from staff and how to keep the initiative from appearing to be a system imposed from above.

With the RCLS's annual staff-development day quickly approaching, management decided to involve staff in determining the direction of the customer service initiative. Five staff members were asked to participate in a customer service team, which would gather information, recommend a plan to management, and plan a kickoff program for Staff Day to be held in July 2005. The team members researched their topic in a number of ways, including surveying staff to determine what tools they felt were needed to better serve the public and improve morale, visiting the Cerritos Library to learn about that library's Wow Service model, and reading literature of customer service. The result of the team's research was to propose a new model for customer service in Riverside County: STARS Service. The five-point acronym of STARS would be easy to remember and applicable to all staff:

- S—Smile
- T—Talk to them (the customers, that is). Borrowing a practice from Wal-Mart, the library suggested a rule of thumb of offering assistance to anyone within ten feet.
- A—Attitude
- R—Response (including how to take complaints and how to respond to customer needs)
- S—Satisfaction

The management team immediately recognized the potential impact of this catchy, easy-to-remember, and highly flexible model. To roll out this new model of customer service, the customer service team (soon to be renamed the "STARS Service Team") planned a program at the annual staff day that combined a report on the results of the survey with a description of the team's findings. The points of the STARS model were illustrated with hilarious and energetic skits that greatly appealed to staff. The team's message was much better received than had it been introduced "top-down" by management, but management was on hand to reemphasize the message. Also, a noted national expert on customer service was present to assist with the program, to set the stage, and to reassure the staff on the importance of this sort of program.

The result was a resounding success. Many Staff Day attendees cited the customer service model as their favorite element of the day. Management—in ongoing collaboration with the STARS Service Team—has begun to put in place elements of the systemwide customer-respone planning that it envisioned but with a high level of buy-in from the staff.

At the time of this writing, the STARS Service Team, in consultation with the management team, is investigating ways to incorporate customer feedback, employee feedback, and service data into a continuous-learning model to improve customer service in the Riverside County Library System.

---

because umbrella institution management will measure success not only by your library or departments, or by staff satisfaction and learning, but also by customer satisfaction during that specific staff day and the numbers of complaints received during that day.

Overcoming Staff-Day Challenges

As you and your staff-day team begin to plan your event, you should consider the following challenges. (These considerations may be more acute for larger libraries than for smaller ones but should be considered regardless of the library's size.)

- *Have something for everyone.* One of the biggest challenges in staging a successful staff day will be to provide content that appeals to all library workers across job classifications. What managers find useful will not necessarily be useful to pages, library assistants, or volunteers. Indeed, the tendency will be to provide programming that is more useful to professional and paraprofessional staff, but reaching pages and clerical staff is key to success. When providing customer service content, it is essentail to get buy-in from everyone; therefore, it is critical to consider ways to make the message relevant to and believable by clerical, page staff, and—regardless of responsibilities —all volunteers.

- *Break up the monotony.* Providing a variety of formats during the day will help to make the day more enjoyable, which, in turn, will help make the content remain in the participants' minds. If customer service training is a component of your presentation, it may be necessary to do part of that training in plenary sessions with all library workers, but devices like break-out groups, discussion groups, role-playing, and skits can help relieve the boredom, not to mention the tension associated with learning a new procedure or process.

- *Focus on quality.* Avoid the trap of believing that you have to pay a lot for quality programming. As mentioned above, you may find that you have experts on your own staff or among the staffs of neighboring libraries. For nonlibrary-specific programs—which customer service often is—quality speakers may be found through local businesses, service organizations, or education groups. And if an outside speaker is used, it is advisable to discuss in detail the message that person should deliver. Most speakers will tailor their remarks to the needs of the event.

- *Do not do too much.* It is easy for managers approaching their first, or any, training day to make the mistake of cramming too much content into the day. Doing this, however, will create too many conflicting messages, cause fatigue in some staff, and generally make staff day a chore rather than an enjoyable experience. It may be much better to focus on delivering a few messages in depth than to try to make up in one day for years of lack of training. Another content concern involves how content matches venue. Staff-development day is the venue for training and education for service-critical, basic, and required-for-all-levels content delivery, and customer service and technology are two such areas.

- *Keep it practical.* Providing training that is meaningful for everone depends on knowing what needs are and meeting those needs with the most practical information possible. This is an exercise that benefits all staff and volunteers because it helps managers identify with the needs of staff and volunteers and make concerted efforts to provide the needed training. As in other training situations, the success of customer service training will depend on the extent to which the training provides the practical tools staff need to provide excellent service. Devices such as roll-playing, scripts, and policy interpretation will provide practical resources to use in working with the public.

- *Aim for best effect.* Abraham Lincoln knew that one could not please all the people all the time, and your staff-development day will inevitably fail to appeal to everyone. Avoid worrying about it. The goal is not to please everyone, but rather to provide a training opportunity that most will find rewarding and that will move you strategically forward in your efforts to provide your staff with the tools they need to better serve the public.
- *Remember to plan to "advertise" your staff day to your customers* in such ways as providing pre-event signage, signage on the day, recommendations for service and assistance for customers while the library is closed, and notification of when customers can expect the library to open again as well as how you will handle customer needs left by message during your hours closed.
- *Have fun!* Remember to keep the staff-development day light. Take advantage of the opportunity to have fun with your staff and volunteers and to build morale.

7

Instituting Continuous Learning in Libraries

Various dictionaries define *learning* as "to gain knowledge or understanding of or skill by study, instruction, or experience" (Allwords.com, 2003), "to come to be able," "to come to realize," and "to come to know" (Merriam-Webster Online, 2005–2006). Learning is very much in the forefront of today's culture. There are learning centers and learning organizations, active and accelerated learning environments, and, of course, continuous learning. Today's "world of learning" is enormous. Researching *learning* on the web finds millions of pages where learning is the focus, as well as hundreds of groups concerned with learning and learning issues.

Learning is good for people. Learning keeps the brain active; people are encouraged to learn throughout their lives. Just as individuals are born with learning mechanisms, which pattern them through youth, and then learn throughout their adult life, this learning, for the most successful employees, should also stay continuous through the work environment.

It is difficult to define exactly what makes people learn, either at home or at work. In fact, characteristics and factors that influence learning can include: linguistic and physical characteristics; cultural and racial factors; the age, gender, and academic skills of the learner; learner preferences; and, most obviously, an individual's learning style. Definitions of learning styles typically describe how individuals process and apply the information and knowledge around them, and all definitions or attempts to categorize individuals as learners are in an effort to answer the questions What type of learner are you? and, therefore, What type of teaching will work with you and for you?

The most commonly cited learning style categorizes group learners as "Auditory learners (A)," "Visual learners (V)," or "Kinesthetic/tactile learners (K)," and these categories of learners often include descriptions of learners' reasoning styles and learning preferences or choices such as preferred timing, format, and environment (Clark, 2000).

Experts agree (along with common sense) that considering learning style is as important as identifying an individual's preferences and habits, prior knowledge, and intelligence. Research has shown that motivation typically affects learning the most, that prior knowledge can be increased by education to increasing learning, and that motivation can be affected by sensitization (activities that prepare library workers emotionally). Trainers and educators should consider and plan for prior knowledge, intelligence, and motivation and then (most important) as managers attempt to integrate continuous learning into the workplace, identify and match teaching and content presentation to learning styles.

Defining Continuous Learning

Continuous learning is ongoing learning. Over the past decade continuous learning has become a commonplace goal, or the standard to achieve, in many organizations (McNamara, 2001–2003). Excellent continuous learning content must be systematically designed and developmentally appropriate and can be general learning needed for performing specific job functions as well as general learning for workplace orientation; training on policies, processes, and procedures for job functions; and general and specific staff or professional development. Continuous-learning content can be presented formally or informally, in-person or virtual, with the format, timing, and location offered with choices to complement employee learning styles and preferences.

Why Adopt a Continuous Learning Model for Work Environments?

Work environments today are moving at a rapid pace. This rapid pace represents business as usual moving faster than ever before, but also workplaces now experience constantly changing customers, dramatically changed products and policies, and procedures needing revision to address these new issues. As the world of work swirls with the different and the new, managers can no longer rely on the traditional one-size-fits-all staff-development print-based or traditional classroom model program of basic or general training with some advanced or specialized training. Instead managers must identify the critical educational components needed for orienting, training, and developing employees for their evolving positions in evolving organizations.

Given the nature of much of today's changes and of projections of tomorrow's changes in the areas of technology, knowledge and information, and security, and given how we have done business in the past, some say libraries may be experiencing more change than many other organizations. Librarians have to juggle new responsibilities with existing ones, leading to excessively long hours and broad job descriptions as well as new work responsibilities, such as teaching, learning, and training. In libraries, continuous learning can become a part of these new responsibilities of teaching, learning, and training; orientation, training, and development; and a focus on delivery and marketing of library services. This division of continuous learning into the three elements of orientation, training, and development is critical to the design and delivery of continuous-learning content and the success of the institution.

ORIENTATION

For new employees or employees new to a specific area of the organization, orientation enables an employee to get in sync with the organization as a whole and with his or her own functional area (department). Successful orientation has the following characteristics:

- It should be geared to new employee performance or probation.
- It takes place in logical increments and is not just a single activity (in the first day, first week, or first month).
- It should involve the entire organization.
- It should include forms or processes that are measurable.

Further and effective orientation should include elements such as the following:

- Workplace or environment tour;
- Administrative issues such as paperwork, insurance coverage, benefits, emergency situations;
- Office policies such as basic job information (description, evaluation, reportage documents, workplace calendars, and organization mission);
- Personnel guidelines, including days off, simple procedures, and expectations of adult behavior;
- Workplace tools such as forms, documentation, and learning information.

TRAINING

Training differs from orientation in that training instructs employees so that they may become qualified and competent to complete a given set of tasks. Separating the orientation of new employees from training is a necessity because training provides both general and specific work responsibility education. Training provides employees the competencies they need to be successful in their specific positions. Training is a change in skills and abilities, and the methods for conducting orientation and training differ.

STAFF OR PROFESSIONAL DEVELOPMENT

Also called the organization's education program, this is a function of an organization that strives to improve staff and volunteer knowledge levels and also perhaps changes in attitudes or values. Continuous-learning staff-development library programs include the following critical elements:

- All library workers are responsible for and evaluated on maintaining their necessary and required involvement in the training, education, and development activities of the organization.

- All library workers participate in ongoing basic training activities that relate to their job duties and performance.
- All library workers are responsible for active participation in assessment to determine their own needs as well as the organizational needs.
- All library workers are responsible for proactively communicating their learning needs not otherwise determined by responding to management questions or surveys. Staff and volunteer reporting and communication responsibilities should include reporting the results of their learning activities for their performance and sharing content learned with peers in general as well as within specific programs such as new employee orientation, mentoring, and partner- or peer-training projects. Also, all workers are involved with the general orientation of new workers, and all staff and volunteers are responsible for knowledge of the organizational structure regarding training, education, and development.

Which Staff Members Are Responsible for Training, Education, and Development?

Although organizations should add responsibilities for teaching and learning into all job descriptions, processes for continuous learning in organizations of all sizes need to be articulated. While some of the processes obviously work best or only in the largest organizations, others work in medium-sized organizations. The smallest organizations as well need to identify how they will manage the continuous-learning process. Choices for continuous-learning responsibilities can include:

- *Training/Education/Development Specialists.* These staff positions typically have all or a major part of their job devoted to teaching, training, and education. They also may assess, track, measure, and report on the staff-development program. (Large and medium-sized libraries.)
- *Staff-Development Council.* Councils are advisory bodies to the organization. They meet and review data, advise on assessment and direction, assist in evaluation of the training and development content, or project future trends. Council members do not, however, work on projects; divide up training, education, and development activities; or assist in support. If organizations have a large number of volunteers, councils may also have volunteers as planning members. (Large and medium-sized libraries.)
- *Coaches.* Typically project-oriented, coaches are identified for their content or knowledge and their skill in working with staff to get the job or process done. (Large, medium-sized, and small libraries by using employees, volunteers, Friends, system or consortia staff or consultants, and so forth.)
- *Train the Trainer.* Although this is typically thought of as a process instead of a position, conveying information learned to other staff will become the responsibility of someone on staff. This person's job is to specialize in preparing other staff for either one-on-one or group roles in instruction

and assistance. He or she is helpful to all staff-development job functions even if the person is not responsible for teaching. This position can educate all staff-development staff in how to work with those coming to them for assistance. (Large, medium-sized, and small libraries by using employees, volunteers, Friends, system or consortia staff, or consultants, and so forth.)

- *Peer Coaching.* Coaching between or among employees of similar competencies, education, or experience—rather than experts or the "coach" listed above—is particularly effective for learning skills and abilities related to the workplace. (Large, medium-sized, and small libraries by using employees, volunteers, Friends, system or consortia staff, or consultants; volunteer peer coaches work well in training other volunteers.)
- *Staff-Development Committees or Teams.* These groups are working groups intended to aid in designing and maintaining the staff-development activities of the organization. (Large, medium-sized, and small libraries by using employees, volunteers, Friends, system or consortia staff, or consultants, and so forth.)

Whether organizations choose one or more of the positions or processes above or do not choose to identify and define multi-staff levels, at the very least they should identify employees or individuals as content and design experts. Other areas of importance in staff development programs include identifying staff to assist in providing input that helps identify performance gaps; clarifying training needs and assisting in mapping out an approach; reviewing, revising, or organizing content or supplying the content; offering ideas for those designing content; and, reviewing content for accuracy and completeness. A growing area of staff development is content designers to facilitate the needs-assessment process; define target training needs and map out an approach; work with content specialists to find appropriate content; organize, design, or script the content; review content for consistency and clarity; and assure matching of audience styles to delivery and techniques.

Individual departments or units within the library often need to focus unique attention on staff development. The departments that need special focus include general reference, where a great concentration and concern for excellence in customer services can be found; technology support; and any special customer services to special-needs groups. Unique focuses are critical where the greatest areas of change can be found; the services provided, such as technology support services, are specialized and typically not in the general competencies needed of all staff members; and, the customers need special attention or unique services.

Continuous Learning versus More Traditional Workplace Training: How Do They Differ?

Traditional workplace training provides orientation and basic, advanced, and sometimes unique job-specific training for employees. Typically, workplace training is offered in standard chunks of information; that is, all employees or similar job groups receive the same training workshop or the same handouts. While aspects of workplace training should be replicated in continuous-learning programs, standardized workplace training does not offer the diversity needed to meet the widest variety of both employee and customer needs.

But what do you "save" from workplace training? All workers hearing the same information at the same time get content consistency; shared learning experience; and opportunities to raise questions, address common problems, and discuss responsibilities and organizational standards. General handouts can match employee outcomes and evaluations, and general exercises, group practice, and scenarios can illustrate organizational standards.

Continuous learning offers the best of the staff-development and training worlds. It includes:

- Basic content, advanced content, and content tailored to meet unique needs, including employee needs and customer needs
- A general program delivering content with follow-up learning opportunities, including e-mails, listserv discussions, tutorials, and learning at library workstations
- Basic handouts to address general needs and handouts in a variety of formats to meet individual needs (where appropriate, handouts should include space to allow staff to personalize the material to fit their learning styles and to create scripts tailored to individual situations)
- Handouts delivered in different formats for access beyond standardized learning sessions
- Handouts delivered on different learning levels, in different languages
- A variety of group-learning opportunities such as learning partners, small group, large group, workshop

Applying Continuous Learning to Libraries

All types and sizes of libraries must pay attention to their orientation, training, and staff- or professional-development programs. Whether the library is a public, academic, school, or special library; whether the workplace is a large or small library; and no matter the organizational structure or culture, continuous learning is possible.

Type of Library

PUBLIC LIBRARIES

The continuous learning processes in public libraries—set within government structures—are often guided by the umbrella organizations, such as the county or city government. Although the primary focus in cities and counties includes the broadest range of training and development, public libraries typically focus on customer service and on those related services unique to libraries, such as the reference interview. All sizes of public libraries struggle with training and development for all levels of staff and volunteers, but budgets for these critical support functions—often identified as "travel money"—are often the first to be cut. The largest public libraries will often have full-time staff or at least part-time staff devoted to training; however, many, perhaps most, other public libraries are in the exploration stages of designing a continuous-learning program, primarily through group-training opportunities and working within state and consortia opportunities.

ACADEMIC LIBRARIES

Although most people think that academic libraries—set within educational institutions—have fully committed to the continuous-learning process, implementing the full process is a struggle of finances, time, and content priorities. Academics struggle, as others do, with keeping up with technology training and customer training, specifically, information literacy. Training and development funding—also identified as travel money—has been reduced, and many institutions ask that academic librarians focus on internal rather than external learning opportunities. Academic libraries, however, tend to provide a wider variety of formats and content, including self-directed content, and have extensive Web presence for staff development.

SCHOOL LIBRARIES

The continuous-learning process in schools is as individually handled as is the site-based management process. In general, however, schools usually have organized training and development through school district coordination, integrated with the content, schedule, and specific needs of classroom teachers. The K–12 environment is also—as is the higher education academic environment—committed to curriculum-based information literacy training for staff and volunteers. Detailed school library standards available nationally along with many state standards outline extensive rubrics of competencies necessary for school librarians to maintain their basic and advanced skills.

SPECIAL LIBRARIES

Continuous-learning opportunities in special libraries are as diverse as the umbrella organizations within which they operate. Profit and nonprofit special environments focus on maintaining status as well as on cutting edge; however, many special environments focus much training and development of content-specific areas unique to the organization's mission.

Size of Library

An obvious statement would be that different sizes of libraries commit to continuous learning at different levels. And although it is easy to see that larger environments find continuous learning an easier commitment in terms of staffing and budget support, the reality is that often the largest environments struggle more than smaller environments given the breadth, scope, and diverse nature of employees and job functions. The secret to implementing continuous learning has less to do with size and money than with the development or benchmark adoption of a consistent method of training and development to match a thoughtful and complete assessment of training and development needs.

Organizational Structure

Libraries, regardless of whether they are organized in both simple and complex bureaucracies, have uncomplicated structures for imposing continuous learning. Organized by functions rather than by numbers or location, typically, libraries can identify basic competencies needed by all library workers as well as advanced competencies for different levels and unique or specialized competencies for specific employee responsibilities.

Organizational Culture

Organizational culture is the set of beliefs and values of the organization that, together with events and activities unique to the organization, represent a character specific to the organization. In general, the library's organizational culture is a service culture, a natural for continuous learning in that in order to have excellent service, training and development must be pervasive, continuous, and consistent.

Encouraging Continuous-Learning Techniques

Although many teaching styles and techniques work well for training and development, several approaches work the best for a wide variety of training and development content and for most learning styles. These approaches include scenarios; scripts; case studies, problem-based learning, and case-based reasoning; simulations and role-playing; and active learning.

Scenarios

Scenarios are tools used to envision the future, written stories or statements (typically brief) projecting activities, events, plans, and so forth—the scenario paints a picture of the way things will be. These stories do not present problems to solve; rather, they describe the environment or the client or the service as it will be. One scenario or several scenarios can be developed for one situation, providing managers, staff, and volunteers with context and alternatives for workers to use in discussion and planning.

Scripts

Scripts are prepared statements, conversations, or dialogue that represent the recommended language and approach to use when in specific situations. Prepared information provides realistic content that models behavior for teaching. Scripts work best when we match them to specific environments and situations. Scripts used in training programs are tools to reduce staff confusion, decrease the risk of communication errors and mixed messages, and provide consistency in interactions. They provide staff and volunteers techniques on how to handle reoccurring difficult situations, such as problem customers, conflicts among library workers, and redirecting of workers in unpleasant situations. Scripts can also help staff and volunteers consistently convey procedural information, such as how to answer the phone or move customers among service points. (A more detailed discussion of scripts and scenarios for specific situations is covered in Chapter 5.)

Case Studies, Problem-based Learning, and Case-based Reasoning

Used in many settings but classic in the teaching of management and workplace issues, these case problems or situational approaches are often considered the "storytelling, then learning" approach. Learners are offered a "story," a situation or case where elements exist and problems are presented. Situations or issues are discussed according to specific steps, identification and discussion of specific issues occurs, and a number of possible solutions to problems are identified with consequences. Cases contain description of the situation including a "who, what, when, and where," and then learners attempt to identify "why" and ways the situation differed from similar situations. These techniques offer individualized, or "personalized," contexts for facilitating learning. Specifically, they are excellent techniques for teaching customer service issues, dealing with change, and envisioning the future.

Simulations and Role-playing

Providing learners with the opportunity to participate and practice while learning is the strength of using simulations or role-playing. These techniques are contexts with instructions that direct the learner to actually perform a task or complete a job function. A simulation can be as general as asking one individual to sort through an in-basket, and role-playing can provide the forum for one individual to offer one of the organization's services to another, such as providing reference or handling a complaint on a site found online.

Active Learning

People learn and, if necessary, change the way they do things best and most easily when they actively engage (hands-on and "minds-on" involvement) in the learning process. Typically, most training and educational opportunities in general (libraries are no exception) are often designed for groups, classes, or audiences with most content presented as one-way instruction; that is, the trainer presents and the audience listens. These presentations, whether in person, teleconference, off-site, or onsite, are called talking head, chalk talk, or lecture. These types of non-active, teacher-directed learning situations create passive experiences rather than individualized and active experiences and often lead to less or slower learning—or no learning at all. Although active learning can include role-playing, simulation, small-group learning, peer learning, and case method, most active learning refers to individuals getting together in small groups to learn through targeted discussions or exercises.

Does great attention to continuous learning pay off? Yes! Building teaching and learning into the life of the organization creates a mechanism for designing and maintaining excellent processes to ensure the most successful library workers.

References

The American College Dictionary. (1962). New York: Random House.

Clark, Don. (2000). "Learning Styles," in *Performance, Learning, Leadership and Knowledge.* Big Dog's and Little Dog's Bowl of Biscuits. (September 2005). Available: www.nwlink. com/~donclark/hrd/learning/styles.html.

McNamara, Carter. "Continuous Learning," in *Free Management Library for Profit and Non-Profit Organizations.* Authenticity Consulting. (2001–2003). Available: www.managementhelp.org/trng_dev/design/cont_lrn.htm.

Merriam-Webster Online Dictionary. (November 2005). Available: www.m-w.com/netdict.htm.

Sheets, Rick. "Assessing Preferences for Learning," in *Learning Your Way: A Metacognative Approach to Study Strategies.* (2004). Available: www.pvc.maricopa.edu/~sheets/lmw/asses.htm.

8

Integrating Continuous Learning with Customer Service

Although the continuous-learning structure is an appropriate model for any training for employees and volunteers, it is a particularly useful approach when teaching certain critical skills, including learning new technologies, information literacy, and, most important, customer service. Designing the customer service continuous-learning structure provides managers, employees, and volunteers with the consistency, the specific feedback, the currency, and the context to prepare them for extraordinary service.

There are several aspects of customer service for which continuous learning can be used to achieve great results for the public. To begin with, there are a number of common customer interactions that are enhanced by standardized terminology, such as:

- in-person, phone, and electronic communication; online customer communication
- moving customers among service points
- fines and fees
- unusual or temporary situations such as hours changes, new or increased fees, construction
- policies that tend to be seen as deficits such as "no parking," "limited technology access," "printing," "service assistance"

Another situation that lends itself to continuous learning is the need of many individuals in the workplace for ongoing orientation, training, and development. Continuous learning lends itself exceptionally well to the need for a standardized curriculum and a variety of educational opportunities for all library workers.

There is a breadth of institutional policies and procedures related to customer service that need a standardized and systematic review for accuracy and currency.

The ongoing process of reviewing these policies and procedures is an aspect of continuous learning for persons at all levels of the organization.

The rapidly changing nature of services, customers, and often individuals staffing service points, also creates a need for a continuous and systematic review of critical customer service incidents that occur at specific service points.

Finally, responding effectively to service delivery and issues surrounding customer service exchanges that often occur without speedy access to resolution or access to management requires continuous learning. The concept of empowering frontline service point workers to solve all problems is a critical one in libraries but must be handled carefully to avoid public service workers being viewed as only "enforcing unpopular policies and procedures." While a continuous-learning tenet is empowerment of staff and volunteers on the front line to increase speed of resolution of customer service issues, libraries often have to adapt standardized scripts and employ conflict resolution terminology for effective resolution strategies.

An organization's commitment to extraordinary customer service is from the top down and is one of the most all-encompassing service commitments of the organization (next to technological service and development). Customer service in and of itself is pervasive within a service institution, and for the best practices to occur, it must be practiced by every member of the organization using the best signage, the best instructions and directions, and excellent communication in all formats and deliveries for all ages of customers. In addition, library workers must practice customer service knowledge, skills and abilities, and attitudes within the organization as well (that is, from department to department) to model behavior and provide an extraordinarily good work environment. (See "Reasonable Expectation of Adult Behavior" in the Resource Tools.)

Developing the Skill Sets

As you design your customer service training and development content, be sure that the curriculum identifies those behaviors necessary to conduct excellent customer service exchanges between customers and staff. These behaviors represent sets of skills needed by employees to provide extraordinary customer service. Although a general term for behaviors is *skills sets*, this term really encompasses all competencies that include not only skills and abilities but knowledge and attitudes as well.

When library management establishes customer-service skills sets and knowledge needed by staff and volunteers, these basic competencies should take into account characteristics and needs of customer groups. Knowledge, skills and abilities needed include conflict resolution, the reference interview, and negotiation skills. Attitudes needed include enthusiasm about serving customers, and commitment to service values.

Typically, organizations identify needed customer service competencies in a variety of categories that are then addressed in curriculum and matched to teaching and learning.

Essential

Essential competencies are those that every member of the organization must master. *Every member* comprises both public-service and non-public-service departments and might include knowledge of the customer, greeting skills, basic reference interview, and valuing a service organization. These competencies are introduced in the orientation of all library workers and are among the first to be delivered in training curriculum. Scripts can be used to provide consistent customer service orientation and training for essential competencies.

Advanced

Advanced competencies are to be mastered by frontline public-service workers and can include in-depth reference interviews and handling difficult staff, volunteers, and customers. Although often introduced in orientation as critical to jobs, these competencies are usually addressed in post-orientation training, typically through role-playing and simulation. Again, scripts can be effective tools for role-playing.

Unique

Both frontline and behind-the-scenes workers should master unique competencies, which include specialized job functions such as technology assistance, technology training, and negotiation skills. Unique competencies are usually taught in advanced training and in development.

Matching Teaching to Learning

Matching teaching to learning is a critical component of delivering competencies in curriculum. Customer service orientation, training, and development processes involve the design of content delivery by choosing teaching techniques that match staff learning styles to specific competencies. Examples include:

- Delivery of customer service knowledge:
  - Lecture or workshop—single instructor
  - Panel discussion
  - Visual—video/movie/television
  - Self-directed study or reading
  - Reading prior to presentations and discussion
- Delivery of customer service skills and abilities:
  - Demonstration and dramatization in context of library worker work, customer service interaction, and role-playing
  - Case method, problem-based method, problem solving discussion, and simulation
  - Scenario
  - Scripting
  - Critical incident

- Games
- Presentation/dramatization with audience participation
- Delivery of customer service attitudes:
  - Role-playing
  - Simulation with exercises (in-basket)
  - Case method
  - Presentation/dramatization with guided discussion
  - Critical incident
  - Scripting
  - Role modeling (with directed observation)

Just as librarians can design and organize the perfect library but not reach or meet customer needs because of bad customer service, so too managers can design and offer curriculum yet not achieve success in orientation, training, and development because the curriculum is not delivered in teaching methods that match worker learning styles. The importance of this step cannot be minimized—especially in the delivery of customer service curriculum. Matching provides customized curriculum for all library worker groups, reasonable managerial expectations for all library workers, and consistency that allows managers to evaluate workers based on the organization's customer service standards.

Serving Special Audiences

It should come as no surprise that the kinds of customer an institution serves must inform the way that library workers are trained. This becomes especially clear when one looks at both the dynamics of serving younger audiences and the differences implicit in assisting internal customers as opposed to external customers.

Children and Youth Customers

Working with children and young adults is one aspect of customer service that is uniquely suited to the continuous-learning process. This customer group often receives poor service in any setting, including in public and not-for-profit agencies. More specifically, in places where money and goods are exchanged, children and young people may get good service but are often treated badly— often wittingly—by individuals who consciously or unconsciously favor older customers or who treat children and young people well but make them wait while older customer get attention first.

Providing extraordinary customer service to children and young people takes additional knowledge of the customer, different and appropriate terminology, a review of critical incidents in tandem with staff members who are knowledgeable about this customer group, careful body language and often unique signage, and effective print material.

In reading customer service literature, it becomes clear, however, that most is geared toward providing service to adults in profit-based organizations. While increasing content on customer service contains references to and is applicable to non-profits, even this content is geared toward the adult client. Individuals who work with children and youth, even in profit sectors, need to adapt customer service or continuous-learning content for their own use.

Continuous-learning, unique to serving children and youth, includes many of the same elements as those to serving adults. Those areas unique to children and youth include:

- Number of general customer interactions that are enhanced by standardized terminology, such as:
  - adult service staff assisting youth customers
  - moving children and youth among service points
  - fines and fees structures that may differ per age level
  - latchkey issues
  - after-hours service issues, homework help
  - deficits such as age-appropriate activities (for example, online viewing and checkout of materials)
- Number and range of individuals in the workplace that need age-appropriate education for customer group and the need for a standardized curriculum as well as for specialized training and development for different age groups of customers
- Breadth of institutional policies and procedures related to customer service for children and youth that need a standardized and systematic review for accuracy and currency and a comparison of how adult user policies and procedures relate to those for children and youth
- Rapidly changing nature of services, children and youth as customers, and, often, individuals staffing service points, therefore a need for continuous and systematic review of customer service critical incidents unique to children and youth that occur at service points
- Service delivery and issues surrounding customer service exchanges between library staff—both adult and youth services—and children and youth often take place without speedy access to resolution or access to management. The ten essential elements of successful customer service for children and youth (as well as a similar list for adults) can be found in Chapter 1.

Internal and External Customers

Although traditionally we have thought of internal customers as being staff and volunteers and external customers as the public, today's organizations have a different definition of *external* that includes such groups as vendors, consortia, partnerships, alumni, and Friends groups. Customer service orientation, training, and development will need to consider these relationships. Another critical external customer relationship should be the faculty and teachers in the school, school administration, profit managers, and city and county employees and peers. These groups are both generally and specifically related to the organization and should be considered critical but external.

Welcoming the Challenge of Changing Behavior

To achieve a fully integrated model of continuous training for customer service, the organization must address how staff—and volunteers, if appropriate—will be evaluated in their customer service skills. For a customer service program to be successful, everyone must be on board with the concept. The old bromide that an organization is as strong as its weakest link is never truer than in terms of how we serve the public. A single surly or unhelpful team member will play havoc with management's best intentions, undermine the good efforts of other library workers, and, if unchecked, cause others to say, "Management pays only lip service to customer service—they let old _____ get away with murder." For this reason, it cannot be a matter of individual worker choice whether he or she will follow the organization's customer service model. The model must be translated into clear expectations and those expectations conveyed to every staff member and volunteer. We discussed in greater detail in Chapter 5 how supervisors can integrate into the employee and volunteer evaluations both the expectations for positive customer service behavior and an assessment of library worker success in meeting those expectations.

But changing behavior is not easy. It is not only that old habits die hard—though indeed they do—but also that achieving consistency across an organization, especially a large organization, means bringing behavior up to a new standard. The gap between current practice and that standard will vary for every library worker. Some workers will already meet or exceed the standard, but unfortunately there are those with whom you will have to work to achieve behavior that meets the standard. What complicates the situation is that these individuals are not necessarily problems. They may be quite accomplished in their technical skills and may be highly valued by library management and coworkers for their expertise. Interpersonal communications is a skill, along with cataloging, reference, and children's programming, but unfortunately it is not a skill that everyone has. For the organization to be successful in serving the public and allow those other technical skills to shine, everyone must also possess the set of skills that compose good customer service. For those who do not have that skill set already, it must be learned.

Further complicating the process is the danger that workers will perceive the library's customer service initiative as the latest top-down management whim designed to make everyone's life miserable. To avoid unfavorable comparisons to the Pointy-Haired Boss in the *Dilbert* cartoon strip, library managers and administrators will be at pains to achieve buy-in without alienating workers, driving down morale, and generally creating the opposite of the desired effect on customer service.

In planning how to rise to the challenge of bringing all workers up to a common standard for customer service, a number of techniques and approaches will prove useful:

Involve workers in the process of creating the customer service model. One of the best ways to achieve buy-in to the standards of your new customer service plan is to have workers help to create the standards. This can be done in a variety of ways that range from forming a staff and volunteer team for this task to conducting staff surveys to convening meetings of workers to discuss the need for customer service standards and receive their input. The results of this effort might surprise you. In some cases, conscientious staff and volunteers may be fed up with the poor service that they observe being offered by their coworkers and welcome organization-wide attention to the problem. Regardless of their receptiveness, however, if workers at all levels have the opportunity to contribute to the process at the front end, they may be more able to accept and abide by the outcome.

Develop a simple, clear set of expectations for behavior. We could all do worse than to remember the mantra "Keep It Simple, Stupid." The points of your customer service plan should be something that can be easily remembered and internalized by every employee, from pages to senior managers to all volunteers. And while the plan might mean something a bit different for each level in the organization—for example, community outreach will have much more relevance to a branch manager than it does to a library assistant—progress toward achievement of the core standards should be expected of every staff member. The simpler and more straightforward your expectations, the easier it will be both to communicate them and to measure achievement. Library workers and supervisors will appreciate having a limited number of points to consider.

Allow individuality in achieving goals. You should wish to avoid the appearance that you expect every worker to be a clone of your concept of an excellent service provider. First of all, you cannot achieve that, and to the extent that you try, you will only generate frustration and resentment. People are individuals, and they have to be allowed to apply individuality to their work. So while it is perfectly acceptable to expect workers to look up and greet every person who walks through the door, to expect strict adherence to a script that has every staff person repeating the same welcome phrase to every customer who walks through the door will make the staff feel like drones (and the customers uncomfortable). Staff and volunteers will find the practice demeaning, dehumanizing, and demoralizing. Let them find their own words to greet the public in person and on the phone. While the term has been overused, consider how you can *empower* your library workers to use their judgment for reaching the new standards of the organization.

Institutionalize the expectations as part of the evaluation process. The best way to be sure that everyone in the library organization understands the expectations and takes them seriously is to build them into the evaluation process. In library workers' first formal evaluation after the introduction of the new customer service plan, review the expectations. Tell all workers how they are expected to interact with the public. Put them on notice—gently and with encouragement—that they, like everyone else, will be evaluated in part on their ability to learn and apply the new customer service standards. Ask if they have questions. Discuss any concerns they may have. But leave the evaluation having clearly communicated—orally and in writing—how they are expected to behave with the public. If the employee is failing to achieve certain standards, an outline for behavioral changes can be discussed with clearly stated expectations for change. If library workers are meeting or exceeding the standards, it should be so noted in evaluations.

Give staff time to improve. Once the supervisor has communicated the expectations, workers should have a reasonable period of time to put the standards into effect. Employees in most organizations are evaluated annually unless there are concerns with their performance that may cause more frequent evaluations. While a year is too long to wait to provide employee feedback on how they are doing in meeting customer service standards, staff need time to learn to apply the new standards and supervisors need time to assess their employees' progress. Once you can tell how they are proceeding, furnish ongoing feedback to help guide them in their efforts. And assume everyone will meet the standards until they prove you wrong.

Be willing to provide training where necessary. Requiring new behaviors of workers without providing the training to achieve that behavior is to program for failure. Like any other skills, customer service comprises a set of learned behaviors. As discussed earlier in the chapter, you cannot expect every worker to naturally possess all the tools in this skill set. Many staff and volunteers will require training to be able to meet your expectations of good customer service skills. Sometimes this will be technical skill that the person needs to possess in order to improve work with your customers. In other cases, these skills will be interpersonal skills, notably communications skills. And as we have reiterated throughout this book, to achieve continuous customer service improvement, everyone in organizations requires continuous training. Every employee evaluation should contain a statement of training needs for that employee. The accumulated training needs of the staff and all other library workers as a whole will let management develop a global training plan to allocate training resources across the organization. And while supervisors will have a good idea what training their library workers need, they should not neglect to ask all workers extensive questions about training needs. This will often reveal areas in which library workers feel unprepared to serve the public. These areas of insecurity are equivalent to areas of anxiety that become distractions in providing friendly, helpful service.

Reward good behavior. Remember to reinforce good behavior. Supervisors should be trained to observe and reward good customer service. Avoid the trap of thinking this has to be a pricey monetary reward or nothing at all. Most organizations have a range of rewards to draw on, from a simple thank-you to honors such as employee or volunteer of the month or the year, including raises and promotions. (For ideas on rewards, see *1001 Ways to Reward Employees*, by Bob Nelson [Workman, 2005].) Any of these can and should be used to reward achievement and success in customer service. If your organization does not already have such a thing, you might consider a reward that is specifically and exclusively tied to success in customer service. Again, this need not be a huge expense, but perhaps some token such as a lapel pin or a small gift certificate. Rewards should always be accompanied by a statement from a supervisor or someone in management citing the specific action being rewarded, such as a letter of praise from a member of the public or observed behavior by a supervisor. To be effective, rewards for customer service excellence should be publicly noted in staff newsletters and in meetings to further honor the individual and to encourage similar behavior. Please note that if you work in a union shop, any awards to staff will probably need to be discussed with union representatives.

Look for "teachable moments." Supervisors should always be on the lookout for the so-called teachable moments, when you can take advantage of a given situation to instruct an employee in the right way to be or to use an employee's positive behavior as an example to others. The key characteristic of a teachable moment is that it is transitory. It is a moment in time, and once it has passed, it is lost. So, supervisors should be on the lookout for behavior that they would like to correct, modify, or reinforce. This might occur just after observing an interaction between an employee, or volunteer and a customer, or it might occur when workers bring a supervisor a question or comment. Taking time with the employee to discuss the situation will allow you to take advantage of the teachable moment. Supervisors, however, should exercise caution in counseling staff in such situations. Be sure never to discuss employee behavior in front of any customers or discuss the shortfall of any worker behavior in front of other workers. Do praise workers in front of other workers but not in a way that is critical of other individuals. You can say, for example: "Linda, I really like the way you took that customer to the shelf to find the material she needed. Way to go." But avoid saying, "Sheryl, did you see how Linda did that? You really need to learn from her." And finally, avoid overdoing it on the teachable moment. Used occasionally, this is an effective tool that demonstrates the supervisor is paying attention. When overused, it is a distracting annoyance that demonstrates micromanagement.

Going beyond Common Courtesy

Some people use the term *customer service* as almost interchangeable with the word *courtesy*. How often have you heard someone say, "I don't shop there anymore; the customer service is terrible." What that person probably means is, "I don't shop there anymore; the workers were rude to me." And common courtesy is a critical element of good customer service. We all know that no matter how good a person's technical skills are, if he or she is rude or unpleasant to the customer, the latter will form a negative impression of the interaction. But conversely, you would not want people to leave the library thinking, "I didn't get what I came here for, but gee, that fellow who helped me sure was nice." Customer service is more than just smiling at the public or greeting everyone who comes through the door. Good customer service is the total relationship between the library and the library user. It includes not only courtesy but also such key elements as technical skills, thoroughness, follow-through, dependability, and consistency. Should workers fall down in one or more of these skills, it really does not matter how nice they are to the customer; the customer may leave dissatisfied with service in your library.

Because good customer service comprises a number of skills, the training implications become much more complex. And changing behavior patterns become more challenging. Changing the behavior of workers who need to remember their manners is hard enough to accomplish—after all, manners are shaped by personality and cultural differences, which are very hard to change—but changing an entire skill set, well, that is a tall order indeed. But do not be discouraged. You may find that what you or a customer perceives as rudeness from a given staff member arises from such conditions as stress, anxiety, nervousness, insecurity, or anger. You might find that if you address the root cause, library worker attitude when addressing the public might improve. And while these stresses may be personal in nature, some may be due to work-related causes. If you find that workers seem to be short-tempered or rude to the public, ask questions such as the following:

- Does the staff member or volunteer have the technical abilities needed to do the job?
- Does the staff member or volunteer have enough time to complete assignments?
- Does the staff member or volunteer have enough time away from the customer service desk to perform clerical tasks?
- Does the staff member or volunteer have all the information needed to work with the public?

If you find that the answers to these or other similar questions lead you to believe that the individual is in over her head, you can begin to consider what training she needs to do her job.

Even if you correct about all these environmental factors, you may still find that for some workers it is difficult to correct deeply ingrained personality traits that contribute to poor customer service styles. In helping workers to understand how to relate more positively to customers, ultimately it will become necessary to bring the service ethic down to a personal level. And after all, good customer service depends on the success of a series of one-on-one interpersonal exchanges between library workers and the public. The ultimate goal of good customer service is to create return business—in our case, to get the library customer to return (remember our disgruntled customer who said, "I don't shop there anymore, their customer service is terrible?"). Whether the library customer will return will depend on the totality of the experience he or she has had.

To get workers to understand this, you may have to remind them of the Golden Rule: to treat others as you wish to be treated. Which of us has never had poor service in a business establishment? By invoking the Golden Rule of customer service you are asking your employees to treat customers as they wish to be treated when they themselves are customers.

Another technique that may help is to get workers to make subtle shifts in how they think about what they do every day at work. This may involve reminding them of the importance of their job to society. This should be an easy sell in library work: remind them that library workers are essential in changing the lives of the people they serve. But more fundamental shifts in the paradigm can be accomplished with language. The Cerritos Library in southern California stopped referring to library visitors as either "patrons" or "customers" and started calling them "guests." Thinking of library users as guests caused a subtle but powerful shift in thinking that made each transaction personal and provoked workers to think of ways that they treat the public. How do we treat guests? We make them feel at home, make them feel wanted, make them comfortable. And most of all, we treat our guests with the same respect that we afford a member of our own family. This is exactly how each and every one of us, from pages to library directors, wants to be treated when we are customers in other establishments.

Applying and Adapting Lessons Learned

Total Quality Management, an older management style, focused managers on evaluating all aspects of the organization—and specifically assessing policies and procedures of the organization—to eliminate all problems within organizations striving for total quality in products and services of the organization. Once problems were identified and resolved (through empowering employees to, in partnership with management, solve problems), policies and processes were designed to maintain an effective organization. Identifying problems requires a systematic, continuous process of evaluation of activities and interactions, especially customer service, and content to train workers in recommended processes. This continuous evaluation and improvement of services and activities spun off another management style as an offshoot of Total Quality Management called Continuous Improvement, or CI. Continuous Improvement management necessitates continuous assessment and continuous training for the organization's critical activities and services and typically focuses on customer service. (For more information on Total Quality Management, see "Quality Management" Web site published by Carter McNamara at www.managementhelp.org/quality/quality.htm)

A critical element of the ongoing assessment of services and activities is the assessment or feedback of customers served. Feedback from customers needs to be approached as systematically as the assessment of an organization's policies and procedures and should include methods for gathering data for all customer groups, methods for reporting and using data gathered (see Resource F for samples), and timelines for evaluating.

A variety of ways to integrate customer feedback into training exist and include:

- Using critical incidents for teaching methods and techniques such as role-playing
- Using data gathered for developing customer profiles
- Using frequency of customer suggestions and complaints for design and wording of scripts

To summarize, continuous learning is a model around which to structure staff development in ways that integrate the training into the fabric of all members of the organization. Continuous learning calls on us to think of each phase of interaction as a training opportunity, from hiring, through orientation, to supervisor-staff-volunteer interactions, to formal training programs. Further, continuous learning uses a variety of tools for training, from orientation manuals to scripts to scenarios to formal and informal class settings. When the model is fully integrated into the operations of the organization, continuous learning can cause fundamental and positive shifts in the way that both supervisors and all library workers think about their jobs, the clients they serve, and the purpose of the library and its programs, services, and activities.

Resource Tools for Customer Service Managers and Trainees

Resource A: Print and Web Sources

Customer Service is a big topic—and a big business—these days. Literature or online searches will reveal hundreds of books, articles, and Web sites devoted to the topic. Many commercial resources provide online training or support for customer service activities and there are dozens of organizational consultants that stand ready to advise you on how to improve customer service in your environment. Choosing between these resources can be confusing and time-consuming.

Selecting the right curriculum for training and education is, as this book has illustrated, a challenging but important task. Although there is much excellent content available in print and online in so many other areas important to workplace learning, customer service content is, for purposes of library and information environments, not as available. As stated throughout this book:

- There is much for-profit content, however, much is not applicable to the nonprofit environment.
- Some content is written for application to a wide variety of environments including nonprofits or library and information settings, particularly the *Knock Your Socks Off* series.
- Most Web environments that focus on customer service are commercial Web sites and are designed to offer primarily advertising for hiring consultants and trainers.
- A few Web sites advertise for hiring consultants and trainers but also provide examples of curricula and/or links to a few articles with titles of other recommended book and journal article content.

A limited (but growing) number of institutions and organizations are putting their customer service programs and manuals on the Web.

Although for-profit content can be used in nonprofit content training, trainers should first look for content that is generic and does not address an environment as either a profit or nonprofit environment. In addition, programs that are the most helpful will have content that:

- Is designed for organizations with similar values such as social service agencies
- Includes practical information such as scripts, cases, positive language, and greetings
- Provides levels of information such as basic or general, intermediate, and advanced customer service training
- Offers tips and techniques for twenty-first-century "other than in-person" training, such as Web interfaces and virtual customer service (chat, asynchronous or synchronous e-mail, or electronic lists) as well as telephone customer service
- Can be used to train employees in ways that are specific to job functions in library and information environments such as customer service support for technology
- Includes profiles of adult customers such as new adult readers or special needs such as hearing impaired
- Provides information on serving young adults and children as customers

Print Resources

The following is a guide to print and electronic sources that will help you get started designing your own training program. Materials on customer service in a library environment can be found in LC: Z 711 and in Dewey: 025.5. Several library-specific customer service books are available and well worth referring to.

Hernon, Peter, and Ellen Altman. 1996. *Service Quality in Academic Libraries. Contemporary Studies in Information Management, Policies, and Services.* Norwood, NJ: Ablex.

   Despite the fact that this book professes to be for academic libraries, the content is applicable to other environments and focuses on the more general issue of overall service quality. Although some critics of the work feel that the recommended measurement and evaluation of services section is abbreviated, recommended approaches by Hernon and Altman are considered valid. Typical academic library services are not left out of this equation, but the book focuses on the academic library customer and what the customer encounters while using the library, such as how materials are shelved, how technology works, and whether employees are providing friendly and helpful general and specific customer services. Several data collection methods are provided.

Hernon, Peter, and John R. Whitman. 2001. *Delivering Satisfaction and Service Quality: A Customer-Based Approach for Libraries.* Chicago: ALA.

   Hernon and Whitman—as Hernon and Altman did in *Service Quality*—focus on the importance and role of assessment of customer service. They offer content for all types of libraries, and this book includes training materials for staff specifically oriented to the concept of empowering staff to attain commitment to continuous quality improvement. This book contains a "Model for Improving Service Quality," a schematic diagram demonstrating the continuous-quality feedback loop (pp. 24–5). (Adapted from Marla Royne Stafford, "A Normative Model for Improving Services Quality," *Journal of Customer Services in Marketing and Management* 1, no. 1 [1994]: 18.) There is an excellent bibliography.

Melling, Maxine, and Joyce Little, eds. 2002. *Building a Successful Customer-Service Culture: A Guide for Library and Information Managers.* London: Facet.

Melling and Little and the contributors focus on the pathway to providing customer-focused services in general and specifically to integrating customer service into the culture of the library and information environment. This book is applicable to libraries in general—although authorship is primarily based in the United Kingdom—and clarifies the answer to the debate on the customer service versus customer focus by illustrating that the terms should be used synonymously. In addition, it presents content for any customer interaction including face-to-face, phone, mail, and fax, and all elements can extend to the world of Web customer service. Contributors focus on the broadest spectrum of customer service by including how we serve customers through the products and service we offer; how we establish parameters of service through setting and following customer service and related policies and procedures; topics such as coaching, counseling, and mentoring; the opportunity presented by regular performance review; and the library and information environment conducive for excellent customer service. There is a reference to training employees in quality customer service, with a good section on identifying training needs. The authors identify four key opportunities for training: new recruits, job change, below-par performance, and the introduction of new processes, services, or equipment.

Walters, Suzanne. 1994. *Customer Service: A How-to-Do-It Manual for Librarians.* New York: Neal-Schuman.

Described in reviews as a manual, this text provides valuable, practical content that is applicable across types of libraries. Walters focuses on the organizational culture necessary for good customer service, characteristics of good customer service, and how-to for training employees. Although the content is over a decade old, it presents a good foundation for a pervasive program of quality customer service. Recommended content for in-person and some "remote" content (phone, and so forth) can be applied to virtual and digital services.

General customer service content can be found in LC: HF5415.5 and in Dewey: 658.8.

Albrecht, Karl. 1988. *At America's Service: How Corporations Can Revolutionize the Way They Treat Their Customers.* New York: Dow Jones-Irwin; Albrecht, Karl, and Lawrence Bradford. 1989. *The Service Advantage: How to Identify and Fulfill Customer Needs.* New York: Dow Jones-Irwin; Albrecht, Karl, and Ron Zemke. 1985. *Service America!: Doing Business in the New Economy.* New York: Dow Jones-Irwin.

Albrecht's classic works provide practical information applicable to service environments as well as for-profit environments. *At America's Service* gives a complete look at how to integrate a customer service program throughout the organization. *The Service Advantage* provides such practical instruments as surveys, reporting forms, interviews, and a variety of measuring tools. Taking a continuous-improvement approach, Albrecht discusses how to assess customer service mistakes and learn from them and how to work with employees to create a quality customer service employee commitment. Also a practical approach, *Service America!* offers practical content on how to manage the customer service program through ongoing data collection of employee and customer interactions.

Bureau of Business Practice

This corporate author or "creator" of extensive business and management practice information for both profit and nonprofit environments offers a variety of excellent handbooks or manuals on customer service, including *BBP Customer Service Management Handbook* (1997) and *Customer Service Excellence Achieved II: Blueprints for Action from 50 More Leading Companies* (1992). These lengthy books, packaged in loose-leaf notebooks, give practical information with extensive lists and model forms, examples and samples, and cover both cutting-edge and classic customer service information.

Carlaw, Peggy, and Vasudha Kathleen Deming. 1999. *The Big Book of Customer Service Training Games: Quick, Fun Activities for Training Customer Service Reps, Salespeople, and Anyone Else Who Deals with Customers*. New York: McGraw-Hill.

Although primarily designed for profit environments, this book is very applicable to all types of environments and all levels of employees. The content is designed to provide motivating and stimulating content to assist employees in dealing with positive and negative customer service interactions. Using some of the most recommended instructive techniques for quick learning, these entertaining games offer active learning in role-playing, debate, charades, and brainstorming.

Customer Service and Sales Skill Standards. Sales and Service Voluntary Partnership, Inc., 2002.

Standards for retail businesses as developed by a partnership led by the National Retail Federation. (See link in Webliography below.)

Doane, Darryl S., and Rose D. Sloat. 2005. *The Customer Service Activity Book: 50 Activities for Inspiring Exceptional Service*. New York: American Management Assn.

Doane and Sloat offer basic content on customer service with handouts, overheads, and worksheets for some individualized but primarily group active-learning activities. These activities include learning objectives, methods of instruction, and suggestions on customizing for individualized needs.

Ramundo, Michael C. 1997. *Complete Book of Ready-to-Use Customer Service Scripts*. Paramus, NJ: Prentice Hall.

This very useful book offers hundreds of scripts for interacting with the public, and although these are very much oriented toward sales, many of the scripts could be adapted to the nonprofit library and information setting. Specifically helpful is the material on phone etiquette (see for example, "Rules for putting people on hold"). Another value of this book is the section on how to deal with interactions for delinquent (for-profit) accounts; it would easily apply to library employees handling customer interactions on overdue collections and other money transactions.

Schneider, Benjamin. 1995. *Winning the Service Game*. Boston: Harvard Business School.

Schneider's book contains substantial material on training, including a section on training staff for personal contact with customers, and stresses the need to integrate formal and informal training methods (informal training is "natural, ongoing process for newcomers to organizations"). The content provides an interesting point on the importance of the employee and customer's first contact and lasting impression in relation to organizational culture. Formal training differs in companies according to whether they have a "high," "moderate," or "low" passion for service. Schneider does a good job of viewing problems as opportunities and states that "employees can be trained to treat complaints as opportunities to maintain customer self-esteem and create win-win solutions."

Weingand, Darlene. *Customer Service Excellence: A Concise Guide for Librarians.* 1997. Chicago: ALA.

Although best suited to public libraries, all libraries will gain valuable insight from descriptions of the types of library customers, customer diversity, basic elements of customer service, benchmarks for customer service in libraries service, how employees work in teams for excellent customer service, communication skills, and recommendations on how to deal with customer complaints.

Zemke, Ron; Chip R. Bell; Kristin Anderson; and John A. Woods. 1992–2002. New York: American Management Assn.

For over ten years Zemke has led a number of experts in authoring and editing a series of excellent customer service books in a "knock your socks off" practical approach applicable to both profit and nonprofit environments. This series offers the basics such as coaching, customer service, best practices, and worst-case scenarios. Highly recommended, these resources provide case studies, scripts, and a variety of active-learning activities. Specific recommended titles include *Managing Knock Your Socks Off Service* (1992), *Sustaining Knock Your Socks Off Service* (1993), *Knock Your Socks Off Service Recovery* (2000), and *Delivering Knock Your Socks Off Service* (2002).

Web Environments

Although much Web-based or online training provides self-directed, often interactive content for self-paced work, the world of online customer service content is different. Online customer service content recommended for viewing includes:

- Individual organizations' customer service programs
- Individual organizations' customer service training manuals
- Individual organizations' customer service policies and procedures
- Training and education "meta" sites, primarily searchable, with specific customer service content links or links to supporting content on areas such as communication
- Some general content from commercial sites that can be used as basic or preliminary training

The following sites are particularly recommended:

Arizona State University

Arizona State University offers an excellent customer service initiative in the ASU strategic planning process. Strategic Planning Customer Service Strategy and Strategy Summaries can be found at:

www.asu.edu/lib/library/ulsp/ul2000/contents.htm
www.asu.edu/lib/library/ulsp/ul2000/service.htm
www.asu.edu/lib/library/ulsp/ul2000/servsumm.htm

Awesome Library

The Awesome Library provides incredible resources for training and education support for customer service. Trainers, however, should not input *customer service* but should input terms such as *cultural communication*. Toolkits and cross-cultural communication tips abound in this excellent resource. Employees can use this site for self-directed or trainers can use the content for small group or large group curriculum for training. Another Web site not to be missed.

www.awesomelibrary.org

Big Dog's Performance, Learning, Leadership and Knowledge

Big Dog's Web site is on every recommended list for any training information. Searchable and greatly expanded, this site offers extensive content on how to train in any area, as well as information on training for customer service with almost 200 links retrieved from a "Google This Site" search of *customer service*.

www.nwlink.com/~donclark/index.html

Client Service Standards and Behavioral Indicators for Baylor University Libraries

Baylor offers a first-class behavioral document that outlines management expectations in specific measurable statements. All types of library and information settings can use this list to design a program including evaluation forms. Do not miss this document.

www.baylor.edu/content/services/document.php?id=20578

Customer Service at Cobourg Public Library

This is an excellent library training document that outlines principles and standards of customer service.

www.sols.org/links/clearinghouse/publicservices/CobourgCustomerService Standard.pdf

Customer Service and Sales Skill Standards

The National Retail Federation is a trade association for retailers, and this Web environment offers content on the association's certification program for sales and customer service skills for retail businesses; however, much of this focus pertains to library public service operations. After filling out a simple form, standards for sales and customer service can be downloaded.

www.nrf.org

Customer Service Toolkit

This toolkit is a government customer service manual and a well thought out guide for use by all types of libraries. Among its strengths is its nonprofit content and thorough content including case studies and management guides such as timelines and outcomes and measurement.

www.service.wa.gov.au/default.htm

Customer Service Training Manual

Brian McCotter, program director for the United States Agency for International Development (USAID), has created a 40-plus-page manual with some good basic content and exercises that include a good self-assessment quiz, a case study, and excellent tips and techniques. Consider consulting a benchmark site for creating your institutions manual.

www.aed.org/ToolsandPublications/upload/Customer%20Service%20Training%20Manual%20(Zambia).pdf

Cutting Edge Customer Service Techniques for Libraries: Learning from Fish and Pickle!

From the Infopeople group that brought us the California Library Training Clearinghouse, this Web site is an excellent set of links to a variety of PDF files and PPT (PowerPoint) presentations providing general introductions for teaching and learning about customer service. These presentations can be used as is or personalized, and they offer general information, group exercises, and handouts.

www.infopeople.org/training/past/2005/fishpickle/

Employee Customer Service—Training Information

The North Carolina Department of Health and Human Services offers three courses to its employees; however, all course curriculum is also posted on the Web. These Web lists provide both links to articles and tips and techniques such as "General Strategies for Dealing with Difficult Customers." This content is basic information and could be used as an introductory level and/or personalized for individual institutions for either employees or volunteers. Also linked is a 15-page workbook that, as a word document, can be easily personalized.

www.dhhs.state.nc.us/cstf/intra_training.htm

Entrepreneur

The Entrepreneur Web environment provides, literally, thousands of good links to articles and online training tips for customer service teaching and learning. Although the Web site is designed primarily for the profit environment, much nonprofit or related information is included. To illustrate the good content, one author included is Chip Bell, who publishes with Ron Zemke.

www.entrepreneur.com/

Free Management Library

The Free Management Library offers outstanding content and links to content for nonprofits. These two pages introduce a wide variety of links on customer service; however, several other areas include content on related areas such as customer relationship marketing. This site consistently provides the most quality in Web environments.

www.mapnp.org/library/customer/satisfy.htm
www.mapnp.org/library/customer/service.htm

Idaho State Library

The Idaho State Library has a wide variety of online training content for new and experienced librarians that includes age-level service content—excellent for providing customer profile information—and services or functions training. Do not miss this excellent site. Interested users can search the Web environment by key word or can link to tutorials and content under "For Librarians."

www.lili.org

International Customer Service Association

The ICSA links to a number of commercial and educational resources with one specific link to "Internet Links." These links are to primarily .com content but offer examples of customer programs, free newsletters, and articles.

www.icsa.com/resources/links.cfm

Knowsley Library Services—Our Customer Service Standards

Knowsley offers exceptional customer service standards and also provides, for the local government service in general, excellent pages for supporting elements of customer service such as "Complaints Procedure." Be sure to view these simple, clear pages, which can be benchmarked and adapted for any type of library.

www.knowsley.gov.uk/leisure/libraries/customer_service.html
www.knowsley.gov.uk/your_council/councils/complaints_procedure.html

LibrarySupportStaff.Com

LibrarySupportStaff.Com provides a combination of structured content linked from simple pages to informal sets of links and discussions. When *customer service* is searched, dozens of links are identified. Approximately one-fifth of those linked are good links to articles, tips, examples, and forms. Although some links are old, this site offers a fine list of both specific and related customer service content. Despite the fact that much is not posted on the Web, resources have been assessed for recommendation.

www.librarysupportstaff.com

Service Quality Institute

The Institute is a consulting and training business that has an in-depth Web site primarily devoted to its for-purchase opportunities. "Media Articles" and "Measuring Results," however, are two Web site areas having extensive content that is very applicable to nonprofit environments.

www.customer-service.com/

Southern Ontario Library Service

This is an excellent content-rich site with links to customer service benchmarks as well as data that supports customer service, such as census data and population profiles. Not only is the content good, but also the content placed on the site is a wonderful example of how managers might arrange content on a library training Web site.

www.sols.org/

Utica Public Library. Internet Resources for Nonprofits

This first-class site is a portal to dozens of resources for anyone associated with a nonprofit organization, with much relevance and overlapping for government agencies. See in particular the section titled "Outcome Measurement, Program Evaluation and Assessment" for many links to topics such as best practices, quality control, and needs assessment. This site provides a large number of examples of the many approaches to organizational excellence taken by nonprofit associations across the country.

www.uticapubliclibrary.org/non-profit/directory.html

Resource B: Reasonable Expectation of Adult Behavior

"Reasonable expectations" are by no means the answer to every personnel problem, but they do outline how people are to actually work in the same spaces.

All too often managers spend their time only outlining the work to be done, who is to do it, how it is to be done, and how to measure what is done. While these things are obviously the primary job responsibilities of managers, it is critical that managers realize their workers spend more waking hours with one another than with their family members.

Managers do have the right to require reasonable behavior of all library workers to ensure work-conducive, safe, comfortable, and harassment-free work environments for staff, volunteers, and managers.

Does this happen already or happen naturally? Often not. Managers, staff, and volunteers have been describing situations at work for years   and often labeling them as difficult and even intolerable. Recognizing such potential problems and understanding how to respond to them are crucial parts of providing customer service training.

Listed below are issues that include patterns of behavior, lists of common, general problems, reoccurring bad behaviors, and content for establishing basic standards or norms for behavior.

Common Interpersonal Problems and Customer Service Issues	
• a basic dislike of each other • an inability to work together • penchants for ignoring all workers or specific library workers • rude behavior • excessive assertiveness and aggressiveness against other workers	• gossiping and spreading rumors (truthful and untruthful) • passive-aggressive behavior • sabotage of work product • overt hatred • destructiveness

Fundamental Categories of Reasonable Expectations
• "common courtesies" such as acceptable greetings among all library workers, verbal rudeness, rudeness by omission, and listening in one-on-one and group settings
• "environmental issues" such as temperature of work location, comfort and preference issues such as blinds open or closed and noise levels, shared work spaces, small work spaces, shared hardware and software
• "work relationships and values" such as respect for the person, respect for the work product, work ethic and disparate work values
• "how work or business gets done" such as valuing diverse work styles, understanding and misunderstanding different ways of communicating, work flow, energy and peak-productivity patterns
• "emotional issues as they relate to work" such as handling criticism, personal issues affecting work productivity and how to deal with the result of personal problems interfering, dislike of fellow workers owing to work-related issues, dislike of fellow workers owing to unexplained personal issues (workers who are negative reminders of nonwork relationships, and employees with habits including personal traits such as voice and laughter as well as habits such as smoking)

"Reasonable Expectation" Standards

- Managers, staff, and volunteers have the right to expect all library workers to behave as adults.
- Managers and library workers should work together to outline what adult behavior should be in work environments.
- Adult behavior expectations can and should be put in writing and addressed in employee evaluations even if only under existing broad categories such as "communication" or "works well with others."
- "Reasonable expectations" will vary from location to location, and there may be a general document with sections specific to certain areas where the physical location or the work functions may dictate different needs.
- "Adult behavior" lists should be determined by first consulting with library workers themselves.
- Managers, given worker "adult behavior" input, determine what are reasonable expectations, what constitutes a violation or unmet expectations, and how to document and improve nonadult or unacceptable behaviors as well as a reportage/evaluation structure and process.

Examples of Greetings and Common Courtesies

1. Please begin the workday by greeting all workers and by responding to workers who greet you.
2. It would not be necessary or expedient to expect workers to continue to greet one another each time they meet during the day.
3. Library workers should hold doors open or assist other workers as needed in similar situations.
4. Library workers should use common courtesies such as "please" and "thank you."
5. Please follow the communication guidelines and include all recipients in necessary communiqués such as e-mails and memos.
6. Although work spaces are tight and we have many common work areas, please inform others when you need privacy and respect others' privacy when working alone or working in groups.
7. While library policy will stress the importance of protecting customer confidentiality and provide procedures to do so, it is critical that those same standards be applied to personal or tangentially related work information sharing as well.
8. Workers should observe those recommendations for communication that include:
   - taking personal statements out of work-related (and other) critical or evaluative information
   - using the standard communication forms for critiquing other work-group or team products
   - sharing all relevant and needed information based on the communication chart to avoid organizational secrets or non- or untimely disclosure of needed work-related information
   - giving all necessary and appropriate credit where credit is due
   - giving positive feedback as appropriate and needed and in a timely manner

---

Resource C: Customer Service Environment Assessment

Today's customer service program includes a concern for the customer environment. Those exploring customer service issues and the design of a program of excellence should not be dissuaded from pursuing excellence because their environment is a "fixed" space either owing to the facility itself or because it is rented and cannot be changed. Other elements that could prevent altering the environment include no money for remodeling, no funds for furniture, or the impossiblity of moving furniture around to better meet customer needs. The first step toward making customer environments more conducive to extraordinary customer service, however, is identifying what libraries do and do not have control over to be able to—in the absence of funding for changes—deal with the issues and design the most appropriate signage or write the best scripts. For example, if you cannot change the lack of style and ambiance in the neighborhood and the library is undistinguishable from neighboring buildings, then managers might provide different external signage, external colors, or outdoor art, unusual sidewalks; or diverse landscaping or plants for both identifying and attracting customers. In addition, realization of the lack of external style might dictate scripts for initial greetings, answers to phone questions, or instructions for directing customers through your Web environment. Also, clever uses of the Web—such as a Web environment that says, "this is what we look like, but this is what we want to look like . . . our digital image . . . how we see ourselves"— offer opportunities for providing a variety of venues for ambiance and style.

Use the following tables for assessment and "circle all that apply." Share results with administration and customer service planning groups. For interesting data, have internal library workers complete tables independently from one another, or have external workers or community members complete tables independent of staff and management—compare data. While table choices may appear obvious, capturing varying opinions and likes and dislikes adds depth to gathering the data. What one person likes or what one person thinks is your "image" is often not what another person likes or thinks is your image!

Styles

Assessing styles of the community gives managers information as to what environments customers might be accustomed to or comfortable with. When buildings are built or business environments are decorated, research is done to determine what styles attract or interest customers and which ones bring customers in to use services. Styles of buildings also convey the message or mission of the services of the building.

Element	Critical to Success	Your Library?	Your Library?	Your Library?
Building Style	Scan of the neighborhood building styles; building is consistent with or blends with neighboring buildings.	There is no neighborhood and/or no neighborhood style.	It is not possible to change the style of the building.	A scan of the neighborhood has been planned or completed.
Image/ Inviting	Building's exterior image is inviting and welcoming to the public.	The building is neither inviting nor welcoming to the public.	It is not possible to change the exterior of the building.	Building exterior has been assessed for needed changes.
Image/ Values	Building exterior communicates the values of the library and of the community.	Building exterior does not communicate the values of the library and community.	The values of the library and community have not been articulated.	The building exterior has been assessed, and no changes are needed or plans are under way to make changes.
Safety/ Comfort	Approaches and entryways to the building are easily navigated, inviting, and welcoming.	Approaches and entryways to the building are not easily navigated, inviting, or welcoming.	Approaches and entryways are unsafe for customers.	Approaches and entryways need assessment by an ADA specialist for recommended changes and cost estimates.

(cont'd.)

Element	Critical to Success	Your Library?	Your Library?	Your Library?
Furniture Styles	Furniture styles fit into the style chosen for the building and thus into the neighborhood.	Furniture styles do not fit into the style chosen for the building and thus into the neighborhood.	There is not a consistent style of library furniture, and one is desired.	Furniture has been assessed for needed changes and cost estimates.
Image/ Formality	The building is consistent with the style of the community, that is, formal, informal, or casual.	The building is or is not consistent with the style of the community and is too... (formal, informal or casual).	The building's image of formality or informality needs to be changed to...	The building's image of formality/informality has been assessed and plans have been made to change to...

Privacy

Ensuring customer service means providing discrete spaces within the library for various ages and types of customers (as well as for all library workers). Libraries as public spaces require a variety of kinds of uses—large-group, small-group, and individual use, including private use by small groups and individuals.

Element	Critical to Success	Your Library?	Your Library?	Your Library?
Privacy Assessment	The library has assessed services and service elements requiring privacy for customers.	The library has not assessed services and service elements requiring privacy for customers.	The library has adequate privacy elements for public services.	The library does not have adequate privacy elements but has a plan in place to redesign or purchase to ensure privacy.
Privacy Policy and Procedures	The library has a policy and procedures in place regarding ages of customers that require privacy and types of privacy needed.	The library does not have a policy or procedures in place regarding ages of customers that require privacy and types of privacy needed.	The library has adequate policies and procedures on privacy for services.	A plan is in place or plans are being made to establish policy and procedure regarding what private spaces are needed and appropriate use of privacy areas by age groups.
Privacy Individual Space	The library has considered whether privacy for certain individuals requires closed- or small-room use or whether private workstations fill the need.	The library has not considered whether privacy for certain individuals requires closed- and/or small-room use or whether private workstations fill the need.	The library has adequate space for private individual space including small-group activity/study rooms and private workstations.	The library has plans for a review of or plans to design/purchase individual private spaces and private workstations for completing library functions.
Private Service Space	Private spaces are provided for customer service interchanges at circulation, reference, and other public service desks.	Spaces or distance between customers and workers are appropriate, without providing too much distance. Customers have the opportunity to seek confidential assistance when appropriate.	Library distances are adequate: Customers at the circ desk have options for privacy when they interact with circ workers. Customers at reference have options for privacy when asking reference questions.	The library has an assessment plan for reviewing and revising as needed, public service private customer service interactions opportunities.

Furniture

Appropriate furniture is critical to age-level services, to technology services, and for creating spaces for programming, research, information gathering, and leisure reading.

Element	Critical to Success	Your Library?	Your Library?	Your Library?
Furniture Styles	Furniture styles fit into the style chosen for the building and thus into the neighborhood.	Furniture styles do not fit into the style chosen for the building and thus into the neighborhood.	There is not a consistent style of library furniture, and one is desired.	Furniture has been assessed for needed changes and cost estimates.
Furniture and Access/ Use/Age Appropriate	Furnishings are appropriate and facilitate use of collection by all ages. Example: Children's room furniture is appropriately sized.	Furnishings are not appropriate and do not facilitate use of collection by specific age groups.	Library seeks improvement to those customers areas not geared to access by specific/targeted customers. Example: Children's room furniture is too big; seniors' area furniture is not comfortable or too heavy to move; youth furniture is too juvenile or childlike.	Age-appropriate furniture and furnishings have been identified with cost estimates for customer service areas including youth, children's, and seniors'.
Furniture and Technology	Furniture for technology stations is appropriate for customer and library worker use.	Furniture for technology stations is not appropriate for customer and library worker use.	The library has mixed furniture including new technology and inappropriate or older furniture and available furniture is not ergonomically sound for consistent use.	The most appropriate furniture to facilitate access to technology (with cost estimates).
Furniture/ Safety	Furniture should be free of safety hazards.	Furniture is not free of hazards.	Furniture is adequate for safety.	Safety assessment is planned for library, and dollars have been identified for these required changes.
Furniture/ Durability	Durability information for furnishings is necessary for longevity and for economic and efficient expenditures.	Durability information for furnishings is not available and has not been a consideration.	Furniture is durable.	Durable, long-lived furniture has been identified with cost estimates.
Furniture Comfort	Furniture is comfortable for customers.	Furniture is not comfortable for customers.	Library has a comfortable/leisure-reading area for customers.	Library has plans to assess comfort level of leisure and recreational reading areas.
Privacy Furniture	Furniture configuration is conducive to good customer service at public service desks.	Furniture configuration in the library is not conducive to good customer service at public service desks.	Library has assessed public service desks and furniture and found it adequate, and there have been no customer complaints and no worker complaints.	Library has plans to assess privacy opportunities at public service desks.

(cont'd.)

Element	Critical to Success	Your Library?	Your Library?	Your Library?
Privacy Furniture Size and Style	Desk heights are ADA-compliant and allow customers and library workers to effectively interact with workers at circulation and other public service desks and complete public service work assignments.	Desk heights are not appropriate to allow customers and/or library workers to effectively interact with workers at circulation and other public service desks.	Library has determined that furniture/desk heights are up to minimum ADA standards and are ergonomically sound.	Library goals include putting a plan in place to bring furniture up to a higher level of ADA standard than "minimum."

Colors

While colors are important in considering style, it is more important to consider colors as critical to setting the tone, supporting services, and laying the foundation to support customer services.

Element	Critical to Success	Your Library?	Your Library?	Your Library?
Colors and Creativity	Colors are used creatively throughout the building and to enhance customer service and customer use of resources and services.	There are no or few colors in the building and/or colors are an older/out-of-date/ style color scheme.	Colors are adequate but do not support customer service activities.	The library is planning for external services (an interior designer/ consultant) to assess with cost estimates possible colors that reflect community groups creatively.
Colors and Space	Colors are used to define spaces.	Colors "cover walls" and neither define space nor create a mood or style.	Colors define some spaces but they are, for example, less contemporary space designations or they do not identify age/functional areas.	Library planning includes a two-year plan for the library to design a marketing/library instruction/plan for using colors to define space and age/functions.
Color Match to Environment	Colors match the environment (for example, blue is a calming color and might better be used in areas where libraries do not want customers to linger, such as circulation, or at technology, where there are limited numbers of computers).	Colors do not match the environment. No cultural or ethnic—if appropriate—are present. Colors are not reflective of community or style.	The library has color and is attractive but is not as up-to-date or reflective of the neighborhood as needed.	Future color study will include a match of library color scheme pallets to the community, neighborhood.

Wall or Space Decorations

Decorating spaces is a design issue and is not only a customer comfort issue but also can be a political issue.

Elements	Critical to Success	Your Library?	Your Library?	Your Library?
Art/ Appropriateness	Art is present in library space and is age/appropriate (if an issue), and all art is acceptable for general viewing.	There is no art in the library.	There is adequate art in the library.	The library plans to display original art as well as reproductions reflecting the community.
Art/Policies	Pictures or murals have been selected according to policy and procedures established by the governing board.	There are no policies or procedures for displaying or commissioning art.	General library policies and procedures include displaying images/art work.	Library plans include providing customer groups to display original art based on policies and procedures.

Noise

In designing public spaces, library planners should strive to mitigate and manage sound and noise to create comfortable areas for customers while not hamstringing library workers trying to provide customer services without "making too much noise."

Elements	Critical to Success	Your Library?	Your Library?	Your Library?
Noise/Service Points	Furnishings and finishes are used to help manage acoustics at service points in the library (circulation, reference).	The library is not excessively noisy at customer service points. There are few/no complaints.	The library is noisy, but mitigating noise is not possible without funding.	A noise assessment is needed to determine what issues/costs are possible.
Noise/High Traffic	Furnishings and finishes are used to help manage acoustics at high-traffic areas such as entryways, commons areas, meeting rooms, and so forth.	The library is not excessively noise in high-traffic areas.	Library high-traffic areas are noisy, but mitigating noise is not possible without funding.	A noise assessment is needed to determine what issues/costs are possible.
Noise/Space/Age Level Services	Library space is designed to buffer sound from areas used by younger customers, such as the children's rooms, story rooms, homework centers, and teaching areas.	Age/functional high-noise areas are not excessively noisy. No or few complaints have been made.	Library areas such as children's areas, meeting rooms, study rooms are noisy, but mitigating noise is not possible without funding.	A noise assessment is needed to determine what issues/costs are possible.
Noise/Equipment	Noise from printers and other machines is managed and buffered.	"Tech" noise is not a problem. There have been few or no complaints.	Mitigating technology noise is necessary but not possible without funding for new equipment and/or buffering resources such as support pads for printers, plants, room dividers.	A noise assessment is needed to determine what issues/costs are possible. Example: A tech salesperson can assess for products needed.

Lighting

While style dictates some lighting decisions, customer service should be a primary consideration in how lighting is handled.

Elements	Critical to Success	Your Library?	Your Library?	Your Library?
Lighting Safety/ External	Exterior lighting promotes safety of library customers; dark areas in parking lots, sidewalks, exterior steps, and other dark/unsafe approaches to the library have been eliminated.	There is little or no exterior lighting.	There is exterior lighting in parking lots.	Library external lighting must be assessed to determine necessary lighting levels and responsibility for lighting/funding.
Lighting Safety/Internal Egress and Ingress Traffic	Entrances and exits are carefully lit.	There is little or no entrance/exit lighting.	There is adequate lighting and few or no customeror worker complaints.	Library entrance/exit lighting must be assessed to determine safety issues/ necessary lighting levels/responsibility for lighting/funding.
Lighting Standards	Library planners have consulted architectural standards for library lighting (see for example, David Malman, *Lighting for Libraries* [2005], available at: www.librisdesign.org).	No standards have been recently assessed/applied (following construction of building) for lighting.	Minimal lighting standards are met with current lighting.	Current standards for lighting for general customer use as well as lighting for technology and natural lighting need to be addressed.
Lighting/ Collections	Lighting is appropriately placed to the shelving; that is, it runs perpendicular to shelving or, if parallel, it falls between shelves	Stacks lighting is not adequate for customer and/or library worker use.	Lighting is adequate for stack use by customers and/or library workers.	Costs are not available to restructure lighting, lighting grids; alternative lighting for stacks should be planned/budgeted.
Lighting/ Natural/ Enriched	Natural lighting is available throughout the building at all times of the day, and glare from natural lighting has been eliminated.	No natural lighting is available.	Natural lighting is available in some areas of the library.	Natural lighting areas should be assessed for use/issues, and lack of natural lighting should be addressed including: purchasing different lighting support; bulbs to increase nutrient-enriched lighting possibilities such as full-spectrum lights are used to support customers.
Lighting/ Supporting Resources	Customers can view library technology or use their own technology with acceptable lighting.	No appropriate lighting is available for nonpublic workstation/ customer-owned technology use.	There is limited nonpublic workstation lighting for customers and/or library workers.	Nonpublic service lighting (e.g., leisure seating) for customer-owned technology (such as PDAs, laptops, and so forth) should be assessed. Changes might include moving furniture or identifying funding for stand-alone lighting.

Signage

Signage supports customers in accessing information and services and supports library workers by offering alternatives to the seemingly impossible minute-by-minute service needs and requirements of a busy customer environment with a limited number of workers.

Elements	Critical to Success	Your Library?	Your Library?	Your Library?
Signage/Style/ Design	Signage is appropriate to the library style. Signs are in colors that allow easy reading, in all lighting, and at all times of the day.	There is little or no style for library signage.	The library has a mix of signage styles.	The library needs a consistent style that matches the décor/general style of the library environment.
Signage/ Labeling/ Library Worker Identification	Signs identify all customer areas and service points. Name tags are used according to library policy; policy includes format and use to balance needs of customers and privacy of library workers.	Labeling of customer areas is uneven and/or minimal. Library workers do not wear or wear few name tags.	There is no signage system. There is a mix of "fixed" and temporary signage in the library. There is no policy on workers' wearing name tags.	The library needs to create a signage "system" and establish a sign policy and procedures for consistent customer service signage and worker identification.
Signage/ Self-directed	Signs empower library customers to find materials and services on their own.	Library customers ask directional questions that might be better answered or addressed by signage. Signage in some areas of the library (general areas) is better than in other needed areas (such as stacks and in library locations not supported by library workers or with workers scheduled intermittently).	There is a mix of signs for assisting customers in locating materials.	Library hours, library workers' staffing patterns, customer service "work alone" areas need to be assessed for presence and success of signage.
Signage/ Nontraditional Issues Including ADA/ Language/ Universal	Signs are accessible by all customers regardless of their physical abilities. Signage is in appropriate languages. Simple instructions with universal pictures are used.	Signs for vision-impaired customers are of appropriate type-size or use Braille; research was done to assess languages needed for signage; universal images are used for high-traffic areas.	Not all customers are served by current signs.	Customer environmental scanning should be completed to determine nontraditional customer needs and restructure signage.
Signage/ Policy/ Assessment	Library policy and procedures exist to govern creation and placement of signage, and policies and procedures include periodic revision for currency and effectiveness.	There is basic policy covering posting of signs in the library.	There is little written policy addressing communicating to customers through signage.	Library policy and procedures need to be assessed regularly and consistently for appropriateness and needed revisions.

Instructions

Instructions in the use of library resources, services, and equipment, both online and in the library, are critical to providing excellent customer service.

Elements	Critical to Success	Your Library?	Your Library?	Your Library?
Instructions/ Public Services	Library workers conduct periodic review of needed instructions for use of library services, equipment, and resources, both in the library and online, including reading levels, languages, and currency.	Library workers do not conduct periodic review of needed instructions for use of library services, equipment, and resources, both in the library and online and/or there are inadequate instructions. Instructions are in only one reading level, in only one language, and are uneven in timeliness.	Instructions in public service areas are adequate.	There is a plan in place to assess and revise public service area instructions.
Instructions/ Service Policies	Library workers are trained to assist customers and use instructions appropriately. (For example, written and/or online instructions are not used as a substitute for one-on-one assistance, but instead to assist customers in the absence of workers or while waiting for workers to assist customers remotely.)	Library workers are not trained to assist customers and do not use instructions appropriately.	Library workers assisting customers may use instructions unevenly.	Instructions need to be assessed for appropriateness in serving customers, matching use of instructions to in-person interactions.

Resource D: Assessment Tools

Libraries have experienced and are continuing to experience dramatic changes. To better explain how we have changed and are continuing to change, it is best to view the library of today and tomorrow in a paradigm shift. These changes dramatically affect customer service and customer interactions. To assist organizations in focusing on customer service, an internal assessment of "where the organization is" in terms of twenty-first-century service and customers issues is found in the table below. Although a final paradigm shift for an organization may have only a "now" and "customer service" column, "then" is included in this table to provide individuals with the context for change.

"Customer Service" comments in Table 1 offer assessment questions for organizations to answer in completing their customer service paradigm shift. Completed tables should include:

- an organization's interpretation of "now" for its organization in the 22 categories (blank rows are inserted in Table 2 for additional personalization
- an organization's customer service elements relating to the "now" categories (the answers to questions asked in Table 1)

Use Table 1 to assess your organization to determine the kinds of challenges that face you and your staff. This chart will help you clarify where your library is on the continuum of change and take you a step closer to designing a training program that can keep pace with change as it arises. You may find that parts of the assessment are useful to individuals within your management group. For example, you will probably want your automation manager to conduct the assessment of items relating to technology. The right-hand column represents various examples to get you started in thinking about your organization.

Table 2 is provided for duplication and assessment. Once you have noted which assessment pertains to your library, you will begin to form a clearer idea of how customer service training can be structured. Use Table 2 to make notes about how your customer service training program can be structured to respond to the library's new or evolving services. Think about not only where you are now but also where you are going, so that you can stay ahead of your training needs as they arise.

Table 3 is provided for duplication and assessment for organizations that feel they have dramatically different "now" descriptions for their library. Your library may be changing very rapidly, or maybe you are a perennial "early adopter" of new technology or changes. Maybe you are pioneering a new service or program. Finally, your library may have a highly specialized mission. Table 3 will be useful for managers in any of these situations.

Table 1		
Then	**Now**	**Customer Service**
1. Most services available only when library open	Many services available 24/7	Which services are available beyond standard hours and for whom? Examples: • Online book/materials catalog for customers with access to computers • Book/materials return for all customer groups • Online magazine/journal access for customers who have library cards and have signed up for passwords in the library during library hours • Online portal for library users including access to "community group," library-use and/or information literacy for customers with access to computers
2. Limited technology for individual use by public	Greatly expanded technology for individual customers	How many workstations are in the library versus how many customers and potential customers? Waiting lines? What time of day? How has the library addressed staff/customer service interactions when stations are not available. Are library Web pages easily used with library staff assistance? If not, are online instruction pages clear? Are 100% of pages able to be used by customers independent of library staff assistance? In the library and outside the library/remotely? *(cont'd.)*

Table 1 *(Continued)*		
Then	**Now**	**Customer Service**
		If less than 100% can be used, which cannot be used? And of those that can be used, by what customers groups? Do special-needs customers have equal access to library technology in the library? Can they access technology independently? Examples: • Web pages available in text? Different-sized fonts? • Instructions on using technology available in different formats and available remotely (audio, large print, other languages)?
3. Customers have more easily identified needs and levels of learning and knowledge. Libraries could identify patterns and thus design services and resources to match customer needs.	Customers have dramatically different needs and are on dramatically diverse levels of learning and knowledge; often hard to identify and change rapidly.	Are library staff familiar with learning style concepts? Are profiles of customer and customer needs developed to drive customer service issues (learning styles, teaching/instruction styles, ages, grades, reading levels, special needs, languages)?
4. Customers spend moderate time with print materials and indexes. Some reading and note taking from materials and much copying.	Customers spend expanded time with library hardware, with little or no note taking and massive printing or copying.	How do customers use their "space time" in the library with resources? Time on workstations? How do they use table space? Few per table? Small groups working at library tables? Time with resources? Printing? Copying? Notetaking? How do library staff assist customers trying to use resources? Standardized interactions for any use issues? Areas? Is there customer signage for work space in the library? Are there instructions for customers? How is customer signage arranged?
5. Offer library instruction in traditional ways such as general or specialized tours and one-on-one; little classroom training or education (in public)	Expanded offerings in addition to traditional, such as distant or virtual, classroom instruction (grant-driven, customer-driven); training is a massive need/cannot all be done one-on-one.	How are customers available for library instruction/information literacy? Individualized? Small, informal groups? Scheduled groups? Where does instruction take place? Reference desk? At workstations? Instruction area? Instruction room? Is online instruction possible? Individualized? Self-paced? Interactive?
6. Single or individual product and productivity workstations	One workstation or network stations that multitask or many single stations configured differently or badly networked	How is hardware configured for customer use? Fixed? Flexible? Can individuals use? Small groups? Can the space be used for teaching?
7. Changes in customer needs are assessed and occur at least annually.	Customer needs change and must be assessed continuously.	Have customer needs been identified? Are data regularly and systematically updated? Is current customer service assistance measured? Are data compared against needs assessment?
8. Change/needs in library services hardware/software are addressed and occur once a year or 18 months.	Change/needs occur anywhere from every month to every two to three months—ongoing reassessment is needed.	Have library staff assessed timelines for technology and technology changes? *(cont'd.)*

Table 1 *(Continued)*		
Then	**Now**	**Customer Service**
9. Strong reliance (by public and staff) on print resources	Strong reliance on electronic and print resources (many customers do not want print)	Is signage needed for electronic use? Are scripts needed to explain, limit, or encourage access to e-printing, such as number of copies? Downloading rather than printing? E-mailing rather than printing? Purchasing disks or print cards? How do reference staff balance use of print and online reference materials in the reference interview?
10. Most things available in print; mainly holdings in catalogs or indexes available electronically	Catalogs and indexes available electronically, much full-text now available electronically, and some things now available only electronically	Are customers aware of online-world versus print world-issues?
11. Traditional services available such as copying	New services added on top of old services such as printing and downloading and basic computer skills such as keyboarding	Are library staff versed in how to provide customer service for all new services and resources?
12. Standard budget categories for buying and record keeping	Additional/expanded categories relating primarily to hardware and software resources	N/A
13. Planning qualitative and quantitative	Planning very data-driven; emphasis on strategic	N/A
14. Planning for resources, annual or bi-annual updates	Rapid change in products drives more frequent updating/greater expenditures	Are customer service polices updated in a systematic and timely fashion to match updating of resources?
15. Limited technology for staff	Greatly expanded technology for staff	Are staff proficient in using all resources available to customers?
16. Not much time spent teaching the tool, rather locating and using content	Now much time spent teaching tool or method of finding, and so forth.	How are library staff prepared to assist customers to use the variety of resources and search tools, as well as the search language and strategies?
17. Reference in person	Reference all over the place . . . in person, on the phone . . . over e-mail or blogs, online chat . . . virtual real time . . . virtual non-real time	Are library staff trained to provide extraordinary customer service in all venues? All delivery methods?
18. Offer only those things we purchase	Offer access to selective resources freely and availably	N/A
19. Offer use/instruction for only those things we purchase	Now must instruct/teach for what we purchase/access/"rent" and then selective resources now "free"	How are library staff prepared to assist customers to use the variety of resources and search tools, as well as the search language and strategies?
20. Administrators/customers had a moderate sense of what we "were" and what we offered	Most non-librarians do not have a clue what we do, what is out there ("Everything is free on the Internet, right?").	Are library staff given customer service training in articulating twenty-first-century library and information changes? *(cont'd.)*

Table 1 *(Continued)*		
Then	**Now**	**Customer Service**
21. Libraries bought/invested in resources/asked for large sums of money less frequently than other areas.	Now ask for large sums of money, much equipment, technology replacement money, new systems and system support, ongoing requests for new and upgrade money.	Are library staff able to articulate, in general, content and answers to questions about costs and balance among resources?
22. Library a quiet place with individual seating for study	Noise! Equipment! One-on-one teaching of hardware/software, vying for seating and finding seats without computers at them! Customers trying to use print materials and computers and finding no room next to computers.	Are library staff educated in information literacy?

Table 2	
Now	**Customer Service**
Many services available 24/7	
Greatly expanded technology for individual customers	
Customers have dramatically different needs and are on dramatically diverse levels of learning and knowledge; often hard to identify and change rapidly.	
Customers spend expanded time with library hardware with little or no note taking and massive printing or copying.	
Expanded offerings in addition to traditional, such as distant or virtual, classroom instruction (grant-driven, customer-driven); training is a massive need/all cannot be done one-on-one.	
One workstation or network stations that multitask or many single stations configured differently or badly networked	
Customer needs change and must be assessed continuously	
Change/needs occur anywhere from every month to every two to three months—ongoing reassessment is needed	
Strong reliance on electronic and print (many customers do not want print)	

(cont'd.)

Table 2 *(Continued)*	
Now	**Customer Service**
Catalogs and indexes available electronically, much full-text now available electronically, and some things now available only electronically	
New services added on top of old services such as printing and downloading and basic computer skills such as keyboarding	
Additional/expanded categories relating primarily to hardware and software resources	
Planning very data-driven; emphasis on strategic	
Rapid change in products drives more frequent updating/greater expenditures	
Greatly expanded technology for staff	
Now much time spent teaching tool or method of finding, and so forth	
Reference all over the place . . . in person, on phone . . . over e-mail or blogs.online chat . . . virtual real time . . . virtual non-real time	
Offer access to selective resources freely and availably	
Now must instruct/teach for what we purchase/access/ "rent" and then selective resources now "free"	
Most non-librarians do not have a clue what we do, what is out there ("Everything is free on the Internet, right?").	
Now ask for large sums of money, much equipment, technology replacement money, new systems and system support, ongoing requests for new and upgrade money.	
Noise! Equipment! One-on-one teaching of hardware/ software, vying for seating and finding seats without computers at them! Customers trying to use print materials and computers and finding no room next to computers.	

Table 3	
Now	**Customer Service**
Services	
Resources (hardware, software)	
Staff	
	(cont'd.)

Table 3 *(Continued)*	
Now	**Customer Service**
Training	
Environment (facilities, ergonomics, signage)	
Library instruction program for customers	
Other	

Resource E: Using Focus Groups in Assessing Customer Service

As an assessment technique, focus groups assist managers in gathering more in-depth content and in increasing awareness of library facilities, services, resources, and needs for group attendees as well as for those who view, disseminate, and discuss focus group invitations. Focus groups can include—using customer service as an example:

- A generally advertised group

  Newspaper, church bulletin, hobby group newsletters, advertisements inviting community participants to visit the library on such and such a day and time for light refreshments and a two-hour focus group (or pick two or three group times such as a morning, afternoon, or evening or two weekdays and a weekend), where attendees—who have either visited the library, used online/remote resources, or called the library—will be asked to respond to questions about customer service at the library. Managers may or may not want to provide programming for other family members during focus group times, and if they do, they should include notification of this in the ad. Managers may or may not want to have attendees RSVP or reserve a place in order to better plan the space and to plan for food and supplies.

- A targeted advertised group

  Managers target specific newspapers or bulletins or newsletters of groups whose readers or members are identified as library users and possible attendees at customer service focus groups. They are invited to attend, and different ads/invitations may be placed in different sources to push attendees toward one event rather than another. Managers may or may not want to provide programming for other family members during focus group times, and if they do, they should include notification of this in the ad. Managers may or may not want to have attendees RSVP or reserve a place in order to better plan the space and to plan for food and supplies.

- Targeted invited groups

  Managers identify groups that they would like to be represented in focus groups that have been library users (online, in-person, by phone or fax, and so forth). These groups are sent invitations requesting that the president, manager, or leader either attend a focus group or send a representative to attend. Managers may or may not want to provide programming for other family members during focus group times, and if they do, they should include notification of this in the letter of invitation. Managers will want to have attendees RSVP or reserve a place in order to better plan the space and to plan for food and supplies.

  Managers identify specific individuals or community members who they would like to be represented in focus groups. Typically, these individuals have been library users (online, in-person, by phone or fax, and so forth) or are familiar with or responsible for some aspect of the library, including umbrella administration managers or governmental authorities. These individuals are sent invitations requesting that they attend a focus group or are sent an invitation with several choices of focus group times. Managers may or may not want to provide programming for other family members during focus group times, and if they do, they should include notification of this in the letter of invitation. Managers will want to have attendees RSVP or reserve a place in order to better plan the space and to plan for food and supplies. Managers should take care that inviting administrators or managers means that groups must be well run, facilitators must be expertly trained, and, obviously, negative content should be honored and handled expertly as well.

The success of focus group activities is related directly to the expertise of the facilitator, the expertise of the recorder, group member responsibilities, and the content to lead focus group discussion.

Facilitator Expertise

Facilitating focus groups can be challenging. Professionals possessing skills in facilitation are valuable assets to organizations, and managers who do not have individuals in the organization who can facilitate should seek community members or facilitators from other organizations to lead groups. In instances where attendees may be asked to be critical or to assess levels of the success of library services, such as customer service, it is best to have outside or nonlibrary facilitators in order to increase the comfort level of attendees.

Although attending one workshop or reading one document can never make anyone an instant expert, basic skills can be enhanced by practice with evaluation. The most successful facilitators, however, are those who have knowledge of the focus group process, the focus group discussion techniques, and the specific communication techniques for managing the group, as well as the complete knowledge and skills required of group recorders and excellent content questions.

FACILITATOR RESPONSIBILITIES

1. Management of the entire focus group process
2. Direction of attendee content and discussion
3. Development of thoughts from all focus group attendees
4. Maintenance of a space where attendees feel safe and comfortable as well as valued
5. Production of usable focus group memory
6. Success of group goals

As with other focus group roles, there are misconceptions on how facilitators operate. As with recorders, there are several things that a facilitator or a facilitated session is not:

- It is not having the opportunity to expound on one's beliefs.
- It is not a passive focus group guidance that involves calling on only certain attendees.
- It is not a discussion where only views that agree with the facilitator are allowed.

- It is not a randomly planned discussion.
- It is not a focus group session where views are presented that represent only one opinion, such as only one way to offer a service.

There are also several things that a facilitator or facilitated session is:

- Valuing all focus group attendees, their backgrounds and contributions
- Allowing focus group attendees to talk much of the time
- Helping a focus group generate ideas and brainstorm solutions.

FACILITATOR RECOMMENDATIONS

- Prepare for the process as well as the content.
- Value diversity in the group.
- Note where gaps in background of attendees occur, and try to get the group as a whole to expand ideas.
- Practice nonverbal behavior that does not indicate judgment.
- Communicate with (if possible) your recorder before, during, and after the session.
- Stress the value and use of the recorder as a focus group team member of yours.
- Focus on—for solution—focus group member clues such as body language showing hostility, boredom, or upset.
- Be aware of conscious or unconscious bias of members, such as gender, age, type of library, or career level.
- Consider using techniques such as "echoing" a person's thoughts back to allow attendees to comment or clarify.
- Build flexibility into your content presentation, so that if one technique does not work, you can switch.
- Concentrate on your primary role, that of listener and interpreter, and give each attendee your complete attention.

FACILITATOR TIMELINE FOR FOCUS GROUPS

Although facilitators develop or use their own style in working with focus groups, some standardized elements in a timeline are recommended for the facilitator's use. Items for inclusion in a sample facilitator timeline for discussions follow.

Pre–focus group time:

1. Review notes taken during any pre–focus group discussions with management.
2. Review timeline.
3. Work out any signals or communication with recorder.
4. Make sure you and attendees have name tags.
5. Be certain that the room is set up to accommodate the expected number of attendees and that changes in numbers of attendees can be dealt with based on size of room and number of chairs, within reason.
6. Review content questions.

Focus group time:

1. Make sure that all attendees have legible name tags with large first names. Gather attendee data by asking attendees to complete sign-in sheets.
2. Call group to order, mentioning the tight timeline—thank them in advance for participating. (If the focus group is a general invitation or ad, query group as to how they found out about the meeting in order to provide library managers with the most successful advertising venue.)
3. Introduce yourself and your role in the focus group process; briefly review facilitator responsibilities for the group.
4. Introduce and stress the importance of the recorder, and briefly review recorder responsibilities for the group.
5. Discuss focus group member responsibilities.
6. Quickly review the guidelines for the group, such as:
   - All opinions are valued.
   - Members should focus on issues of the group and not, for example, critique previous activities.
   - As facilitator, you reserve the right to structure time carefully to reach all questions and to place ideas or content in "parking lots" for discussion at a later time.
   - Comments should be made with a "safe space" disclaimer; do not focus on a member's personality, but on his or her ideas; avoid saying, "We tried that, and it did not work"; ask clarifying questions as necessary. And, more behavioral-related guidelines: avoid ongoing negativism, identify yourself by first name before speaking during the discussion, and avoid getting up, leaving, and returning during the hour.
   - Avoid interrupting other attendees, make written notes of thoughts for later mention, help attendees focus on adhering to the timeline. Participants should expect to do 95% of the talking. Avoid gossip and telling stories with names attached, to protect anonymity; avoid excessive body language to attract attention.
   - Do not engage in sidebar conversations with attendees or the recorder unless your discussion relates to recorder or focus group attendee business.
   - State up front that attendees may be asked to prioritize or revisit other group memories and decisions.
7. Begin discussion with content questions.
8. Touch base with the recorder as necessary.
9. Stop at least a few minutes before the end of the group activity for the recorder to recap and clarify.
10. Create a "closure" with thank-you sentiments.

Post–focus group time:

- Meet with the recorder to clarify issues.
- "Sign-off" on the group memory.
- Consider sending attendees thank-you notes for attending.

Recorder Expertise

Recording information from a group process is also identified as "taking minutes" or creating a, in this case, focus group memory. The "most dreaded,
feared, and hated" role to be assumed in a group—that of taking minutes or
being that recorder—is also one of the most if not the most important group role
to assume. Because it is such a disliked and misunderstood role, it is first important to clarify what it is and what it is not:

- It is not recording every word that is said, exactly as it is said.
- It is not occasionally jotting down important phrases.
- It is not writing down what the recorder agrees with or what the recorder
  thinks the outcome should be.
- It is not using unknown shorthand.
- It is not (or does not always have to be) a recorder spending endless time
  rewriting the content for broad understanding.
- It is not relegation to a totally silent attendee role.
- It does not ensure a lack of involvement or take away a right to contribute.

In most of the literature of recording, "group memory" most often refers to
the recorder's flip-chart-sized notes that are posted on the walls around the
focus group discussion room.

- It is working as a team member, specifically with the group leader, the
  facilitator.
- It is creating an instant group memory that captures not only words but
  also priorities, comparisons, rankings, and the group spirit.
- It is being the best possible listener.
- It is being a participant in the group after stating, "The necessary recorder
  pen has been put aside."
- It is assuming responsibility of any needed clarification and a smooth flow
  of group process.
- It is playing a major verbal supporting role to the facilitator as needed.

Responsibilities of recorders include the role(s) they play; their pre-group,
during, and post-group activities; as well as recorder to-dos.

RECORDERS

1. Establish a legend to explain signs, symbols, colors, and abbreviations.
2. Organize the facts, issues, and ideas to indicate priorities and rankings as
   shown by dialogues as well as by voice inflection.
3. Record the facts, issues, and ideas generated by attendees.
4. Highlight the written record using signs, symbols, colors, and
   abbreviations.
5. Use techniques to organize the information to increase accuracy.
6. Perform (typically thought of as) non-recorder functions in this order:

"Content:

Guiding the agenda; clarifying and rephrasing; keeping the discussion on topic; reformulating the question or problem; summarizing; testing for agreement (or calling for a vote); and Identifying decisions and implementation plans.

Interaction:

Pacing (attention to speed and energy levels of interaction); equalizing participation; identifying communication problems; soliciting feedback; aiding the group's emotional climate; and identifying individuals' emotions as they affect participation (Volkema, 1999).

RECORDER RECOMMENDATIONS

- Use a variety of colors to indicate priorities, rankings, "spirit," decisions, and so forth. Clearly label each session's memory note pages even though notes may be attached. Write as clearly and legibly as possible, use standardized abbreviations as often as possible, use abbreviations consistently, and avoid personal doodling on all note pages. Remain bipartisan or neutral when recording, prioritizing, or ranking; feel free to misspell (it's more important to get the ideas down); familiarize yourself with (and practice) the techniques of note taking.
- Realize you may be adding to the legend as you go as you note repetition in ideas, issues, or key words.
- Consider punctuation as verbal symbols (example: use dashes, dots, periods, and asterisks consistently).
- Consider using standardized symbols (use greater than and less than symbols, equals symbols, parallel lines, and so forth, consistently).
- Use uppercase letters, lowercase letters, and numerals consistently to label or outline ideas.
- Concentrate on listening before writing to capture the differences between main ideas and supporting ideas, and seek facilitator and group member clarification at any point; be open-minded.

SPECIFIC TECHNIQUES

Recording information for later use is a very personal process. Most people create their own shorthand, note-taking techniques at one time during their career and then hesitate to use these processes when recording for other focus groups.

The following techniques include five different ways of selecting and organizing information:

1. Simple list

Simple lists are ideas or key word lists. Their goal is to merely organize subtopics under main topics. These lists are headed by an underlined topic or heading, followed by listed items of information, facts, or ideas that the recorder may choose to number. Attendees may list ideas by themselves, such as, "There arc three ways to do this," or lists can be created by one member outlining a topic and three others following with elements of that topic. Examples of these lists may include "things to do list," "ways to do things," or "brainstormed ideas" for issues or problems.

Customer service examples for recording a simple list:

- *Write scripts for answering phones.*
- *Greet people consistently upon entering the library.*
- *Establish routines for circ workers to identify satisfaction level of customers leaving the library such as: Did you find what you need? Can we do anything else for you today?*

2. Chronological list

Chronological lists are idea or key word lists. These lists are headed by an underlined topic or heading. Their goal is to indicate a specific way that something occurs in order for something to be successful. Any items listed below the topic must be in order and are usually numbered to indicate order.

Group members when listing ideas chronologically use words such as *first, then, next,* and *last.*

Examples of these lists are "how-to" lists and, obviously, "events occurring in a timeline or necessary order."

Customer service examples for recording a chronological list:

- *First—library workers should work on their greeting skills for every customer entering the library.*
- *Second—library workers should seek training on how to deal with teens who "hang out" at the library.*

3. Cause and effect

Cause-and-effect lists have a main idea with additional ideas supporting or relating to the main idea. Their goal is to indicate the reasons why something happens. They can be arranged as simple lists; however, they can also be visually arranged (see examples in italics). Information may or may not be prioritized or numbered.

Attendees may introduce a cause and effect list by using these specific words, or they may say, "That happens because," or "If we do this, here is what will happen," or "I know why... it is because...."

Customer service examples for recording cause and effect:

Focus group attendees thought the reason why we did not get good responses on the customer service survey last summer was because:

- *Library workers did not seem to be "engaged" in the questionnaire process because they did not remind each customer leaving that he or she should complete and return the questionnaire.*

- *Reference staff did not suggest that—post reference—customers complete response cards.*

4. Comparison and contrast

Comparison-and-contrast lists include ideas, issues, information, topics, and so forth. Information may be prioritized or numbered. Their goal is to indicate the differences and similarities between and/or among items, information, and issues. Visual organization is key to easy use of this type of list (see example).

Group members may use words such as *similar, different,* or *compare.* The key to success of the visual image created is consistent use of words on the list.

Examples of these types of lists include "comparison of types" and "highlighting differences for the purposes of discussion, agreement, or problem solving."

Customer service examples for comparison and contrast:

- *The best customer service attendees experienced was at the local family-owned restaurant, specifically for greeting and exiting the establishment.*
- *The best customer service at the library was when customers exited; however, greeting was often spotty, and customers had to approach library workers to get attention.*

5. Mind mapping, clustering, hurricane writing, diagramming

Mind mapping, clustering, hurricane writing, and diagramming are all visual techniques for recording information on paper. Their goals include: allowing recorders to take notes when fast-paced, spirited attendee discussions are going on; creating a visual picture that in and of itself conveys content and possible organization; organizing material more as the whole brain sees and recalls it; and creating a record that is easily recalled owing to right-brain involvement and nonlinear organization. The characteristics of these techniques include:

- Placing the main topic in the center of the page inside a geometric shape
- Putting supporting ideas into two-word uppercase phrases that are strong nouns, concrete, and meaningful
- Placement of these supporting ideas or subtopics on "limbs" coming out from the structure
- Placement of these ideas under subtopics, under the subtopics themselves.

Rather then placing ideas in order visually, members or the recorder may number or use color to indicate priorities, rankings, enthusiasm, and so forth. Other ways of grouping could include all related limbs in similar colors. Recorders are also encouraged to use signs, symbols, circling, and underlining to create images.

Although diagramming and hurricane writing are often used synonymously for mind mapping, clustering may evoke images, similar to the cause-and-effect listing technique.

Customer service examples include:

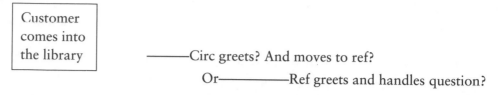

RECORDER TIMELINE FOR GROUPS

Although, like facilitators, recorders develop or use their own style in working with attendees, some standardized elements in a timeline are recommended for the recorder's use. Items for inclusion in a sample recorder timeline for group discussions follow.

Pre–focus group time:

1. Review notes taken at activities.
2. Review timeline.
3. Work out any signals or communication with the facilitator.
4. Get a name tag.
5. Get out your writing utensils.

Group time:

1. Note all attendee names.
2. Clarify any recorder responsibilities as the facilitator outlines them.
3. Interrupt discussion as necessary for clarification.
4. Touch base with the facilitator as necessary.
5. Participate as necessary in recapping.
6. Participate in closure activities.

Post–focus group time:

1. Meet with facilitator to clarify issues.
2. "Sign off" on group memory with facilitator.

Focus Group Member Responsibilities

Being an attendee has its set of responsibilities. These responsibilities should be outlined for members by the facilitator at the beginning of the group discussion. (This was outlined in the facilitator timeline.)

GROUP MEMBERS' RESPONSIBILITIES

- Attendance during the entire focus group meeting/activity
- Commitment to the project at hand
- Understanding—and if not, seeking clarification on—the process
- Enthusiasm for the process
- Participation in discussion
- Belief in the value of all participants' opinions

- Willingness to focus on the issues of the discussion
- Honoring the "safe space" disclaimer of the process
- Avoidance of ongoing negativism
- Adherence to focus group guidelines of behavior such as: no excessive body language, no interruptions, no distracting sidebar conversations, working with ideas and not personalities, and a commitment to a full hour's work for each session
- Realization that although ongoing conflict is not good, disagreement and seeking out differences of opinion are crucial to any complete discussion
- Not changing opinions to avoid conflict
- Clear communication of ideas and willingness to clarify points-of-view.

Content to Lead Focus Group Discussions

Group discussion as a process is used to instill commitment and gather information on ideas and processes by maximizing use of activity participants. Organizations should realize that focus groups often have a mind and life of their own; they may have unique personalities, even if they meet for only two hours; work can be achieved through a variety of discussion techniques; and content questions are critical to the success of the focus group.

WAYS TO GENERATE FOCUS GROUP RESULTS

Although they are not the only ways to discuss or achieve group goals, these ways should be considered:

1. Questioning

Any group process chosen can begin by the facilitator's posing of questions to the group; however, the process itself may be the choice of relevant questions and recording participant response.

Customer service content questions might include:

- *The library's goal is extraordinary customer service. Think for a minute about the most extraordinary customer service experience you have had. Could you translate that to the library environment? If so, how would you do that?*
- *What can we learn from good customer service in other organizations or businesses?*
- *What was the best customer service experience you have had at the library?*
- *What was the worst customer service experience you have had? If it was in the library, describe it as generally as possible.*
- *In your opinion as a customer, what is the most important customer service the library can offer?*
- *Does library signage meet customer needs? What are the two best aspects of library signage? What three things would you improve in library signage?*

- *Is the library meeting both in-person and digital customer needs?*
- *In your opinion as a customer, what words do you hate to hear?*
- *What words do you love to hear?*
- *What was the best customer service response to a conflict you have experienced?*
- *What are the two most important recommendations you see on the _____ (for example, flip-chart, mind map) today?*
    OR
- *Take your (magic markers or voting sticky dots) and vote for the five most important changes we can make in our library's customer service.*

2. Brainstorming

This process has the facilitator tossing out ideas and the group responding with wild, not-so-wild, and even impossible ideas. The guidelines for brainstorming include the lack of evaluation of ideas as they are generated, the lack of recording ideas initially (recorders wait until summary and discussion), a rapid flow of ideas, and a timeline such as "a ten minute brainstorming, then a fifteen minute discussion."

Each attendee should respond to this question: "How would the library use the Wal-Mart greeter concept?"

3. Nominal group (or round-robin)

Members individually respond in some order to specific ideas or issues presented. One issue is handled at a time. The strict definition of nominal group techniques includes options individually written on paper and either a verbal or written discussion taking place for each idea or issue presented.

Each attendee should—taking no more than two minutes—use a phrase that he or she thinks would work as a greeting in the library.

4. Impossible questions

The facilitator structures a question to illicit responses concerned with "what may be impossible...but if we could, we would."

If we had unlimited money for customer service training, what should we offer?

5. Visualization

Group members are given an ideal situation and asked to visualize it and respond, or group members are asked to create an ideal situation and then describe it so that others may "see it," and then the group discusses.

Close your eyes and imagine the perfect exchange between library worker and the most difficult customer. What are the high points of that exchange?

6. Problem solving

The facilitator, an attendee, or the group as a whole discuss a situation or issue, identify a problem, generate a list of options or ways to solve the problem, and develop a plan.

The library needs a customer service program in place by September. What steps should we take to design a program in such a short period of time and with little funding?

7. Evaluate options

The facilitator presents an issue, idea, or problem with a list of ideas, concerns, or solutions; then the group members analyze, reduce, add, and decide on the list or the options presented.

Library signage is outdated and misunderstood. Library workers have generated the following options. Review, discuss, and prioritize what might work best to create new signage.

- Get a local design class to compete in designing new library signage.
- Take a field trip to identify signage in a neighboring library.

For purposes of this process, given environment, time limitations, and preparation, the recommended processes include questioning, brainstorming, the impossible questions, visualization, and evaluation of options.

Much of this appendix has been adapted from the work of Fred Niederman and Roger J. Volkema, especially their article "The Effects of Facilitator Characteristics on Meeting Preparation, Set Up, and Implementation," *Small Group Research* 30 (1999): 330–60.

Resource F: Customer Service Response Forms

Surveying customers for general feedback on customer service typically falls into two categories: questionnaires and response or comment cards. These documents can include:

- interview questions (typically called interview schedules) for in-depth, in-person interviews
- online documents/questionnaires—offered to anyone
- online documents/questionnaires—offered to customers following use or a customer interaction
- online response cards—offered to anyone
- online response cards—offered to customers following use or a customer interaction
- in-person print/questionnaires—offered to anyone
- in-person print/questionnaires—offered to customers following use or a customer interaction
- in-person print/response cards—offered to anyone

- in-person print/response cards—offered to customers following use or a customer interaction

Obviously, managers can gather extensive information from interviews or from questionnaires and can analyze data gathered to identify issues and gaps; compare and contrast content against organizational goals, strategy, or outcome statements; and compare institutional data against benchmark data from other, similar institutions or other, comparable environments that have similar customer service programs.

Response or comment cards, however, provide broad, valid, typically point-of-use opinions, but, because they are are not consistently and systematically gathered data, they typically cannot be and should not be used to indicate trends or changes in customer opinion. Although one might then speculate on the value of response or comment cards at all, the advantages are there, and they do include:

- Offering customers a quick, easily completed targeted use for feedback (opportunities to compliment, complain, query, and so forth)
- The facility of compiling data on cards
- Enabling response to individual customers, confidentially
- Enabling public response—in the aggregate and preserving anonymity—to provide general information back to customers
- Illustrating goodwill to customers who feel, even if they choose not to, you care about their opinions (Should managers wish to make response boxes locked or sealed containers, this also indicates to customers that, odds are, their comments will make it to management and that they can be candid.)

Where Might Response Cards Be Located?

Response cards should be distributed widely throughout the organization including: all public service desks (circulation, reference, information, age-level service desks, and so forth). This distribution should also include passive and active distribution, such as cards near the desks where customers can discover them, library workers pointing out cards, and library workers putting cards in materials as customers leave with them. Active language might include a script that states, *"If you don't mind, please take a few minutes to complete this response card to let us know how we are serving you. It takes less than five minutes, and you can drop it in the mail to us, fax it to us, fill it out now and drop it in the box, or bring it back with you when you return this item. Thanks so much for your time."*

Response cards should be

- in managers' offices
- in public and school library offices of those who interact with children or parents of children, and in academic libraries where librarians keep office hours for meeting with customers
- in or near other public-use areas such as meeting rooms

- posted to the main Web page
- posted to designated high-customer traffic pages
- posted to secondary pages
- posted to a public in-person bulletin board, display, or exhibit area
- staff break rooms
- common-use library worker areas

Response cards should also be taken—by library workers reaching the community outside the libraries—on remote use services such as bookmobiles; when librarians or library workers visit schools or customers in hospitals, community centers, classrooms, school PTA meetings; to library booths at community fairs; and for unusual situations such as when library workers reach out in disaster or emergency situations by serving customers in their homes, temporary shelters, and so forth. And, although response cards are not typically located in areas such as public restrooms, management should consider windows of opportunity when other public areas might be targeted for response card distribution and assessment opportunities.

What Are the Issues Related to the Cards Themselves?

What separates response cards from questionnaires is brevity, so be brief! Resist the temptation to ask all those questions that you must have the answer to, and if you find it is impossible to shorten the response card, consider creating a general response card or a brief targeted response card (only for children's services or only for reference or circulation interactions) and a questionnaire. Other response card issues include:

- Be clear and specific about what you are asking customers to comment on: for example, ask that they state names of services while avoiding library terms such as "checkout" rather than "circulation."
- Querying customers on a service rather than on an individual, such as "Rate your interaction when you check out your materials today" rather than "Rate your interaction with the circulation worker on duty."
- Selecting responses that gather data on what can be changed, and referring to behavior or issues that can be changed.
- Avoiding making any judgment statements, such as "We're having complaints about our Web site! Tell us what you think." Rather say, "We're looking at reviewing our year-old Web site; tell us what you think."
- Avoiding broad ranges such as "all," "never," "always," and so forth. Examples of what you should not do include using words in italics: "*Everytime* I check out books I get [pick one: great, good, acceptable, bad] service."

Examples of Response Cards

- **How are we doing?** A general customer question, "How are we doing?" with one introductory (or summative) scaled response such as "Always wonderful!"; "Usually great"; "Always acceptable"; "A few problems," and an open-ended comment area.

- **Please rate our service.** This can be "service" or "services" and can be as brief as service areas with scaled responses such as "children's services," "adult programs," or public service desks that provide services such as "circulation services" or "reference services." This approach requests the customer to respond broadly but avoids the personal "you."

- **Let us know what you think…** This interjects the use of "you" to encourage a personal connection and gather a personal response. It shows customers you care what they think and that you welcome information. This can be open-ended in general, can have scaled responses, or can have a library worker "fill in the blank" that directs the library worker who solicts the response to fill in the "about" section such as "Let us know what you think about… *the service you got at the IRS help desk today or how you enjoyed the Internet training workshop or what one thing you learned in the information literacy class presentation.*"

- **We need your help.** Typically a "plea for help" is used for targeted or intermittent response card use such as "every fall" or "in the middle of every semester" or "following the end of the summer club."

Examples of Scales of Response

- **General ranges.** Gathering data with general ranges has both good and bad elements. Obviously, good elements include ease of response, likelihood of completion, and brevity of content. Bad elements include data gathered is too general and does not say enough to managers. In addition, ranges with fewer than seven choices do not offer customers or managers much differentiation, and many ranges do not include the "not applicable" choice—in most cases it should be included. General ranges can be designated by letters or numbers that indicate levels (Example: 0 is never, 1 is sometimes, 2 is often, 3 is always, and so on). The most general ranges can have a listing of letters, numbers or marks, with range statements at either end. Ranges should also be clearly labeled as to "least to most" or "most important to least important." Here is an example of a general range with range statements at either end:

Not at all important							Very important
0	1	2	3	4	5	6	7

- **Content alternatives.** Content alternatives—while similar to labeling or marking each number or letter—include more information to describe each number, letter, or mark on the scale. This individualized attention to and content on each range on the scale allows managers to include fewer numbered ranges (and save on space!) and provide unique and targeted data gathering and data analysis. Managers can also target and match levels on the ranges/scales to goals and outcomes. Examples include:

0—Not Applicable. I haven't used this service in the library.

1—I have used this service and have rated it very highly for customer service. (Give us your best example!)

2—I have used this service and have had good customer service experiences. (Give us an example below if you have time.)

3—I have used this service and have a few comments about the customer service. (Tell us why you feel the way you do about this customer service experience in the library.)

4—I have used this service and typically do not have a good customer service experience. (Please complete the card by telling us why you do not have a good experience.)

How Would You Approach Evaluating Response Card Content?

- Gather cards systematically and periodically.
- Code where the cards are picked up to provide a location focus to the data gathered. Create spreadsheets where you can aggregate the responses under questions asked.
- Create a basis of comparison including baseline data from past matching research.
- Create categories of response that can include: outcomes, goals, or customer service areas of importance such as, for example, accuracy, overall courtesy, hours of access, and hours of service.
- Look for patterns of responses
- Look for matches to outcomes and goals from your customer service program.
- Complete a sample, aggregate response card that gathers all information and acts as your organization's "report card." Example:

0	1	2	3	4
Only 10% of respondents had not used the service.	32% rated the customer service very highly.	43% rated the customer service as "good."	12% had a few comments about the service (see comments section below).	3% of respondents have had consistently bad service (see comments attached for that information).

Response Card Recommendations

- Collect sample cards from all other establishments to benchmark what works for others.
- Consider having self-addressed, stamped envelopes for a greater rate of return.
- Create three cards: a general response card, an age-level service card, and a response card specifically for complaints or potential negative interactions.

- Keep the physical size of cards small to illustrate quick-response opportunities.
- Use Likert scales of response that provide *content alternatives* to reduce aggregate, general, and possibly too general, data.

Resource G: Customer Service Incident Feedback Process

This form provides content on how library workers should communicate incidents, or issues or complaints regarding customer service to library managers and other library workers. All those reporting/using the process should note that content completed should be written in exact, descriptive language, but be neutral in tone, and should contain direct quotes—when applicable—to accurately reflect what was said and done in the situation.

All library workers should complete this process if an issue was a difficult one, if the situation has not been resolved and should be referred, if they wish for assistance in resolving the current issue, and if they seek assistance in handling future issues and situations.

Process

1. During incidents or situations, be aware of and note the presence of any library workers or, if appropriate, any other customers who might be helpful in recounting elements of the situation.
2. If possible and appropriate, take notes during the incident or situation.
3. If notes are not possible during the situation, immediately after reflect on what happened and write it down in the order in which the events occurred using exact, descriptive language in neutral tones with, as much as possible, direct quotations. (See examples at the end of this document.)
4. If workers observed, ask that they write their recollection of the situation or incident. If customers observed difficult situations and offer or agree to write a statement, give them the information (name, building, or e-mail address) and ask them to submit their recollection of the situation in their own words with contact information for follow-up if there are further questions or if additional information is needed.
5. If time permits, share your recounting with workers who observed the incident to get their input and comments on your accuracy.
6. Send your completed memo or e-mail to the manager on duty making sure to indicate time-sensitive issues and customer requests.
7. The manager on duty should comment as necessary and forward content to the appropriate managers or individuals, such as the volunteer coordinator, if a volunteer is involved.
8. Managers should respond to library workers immediately to the effect that they have received forms and to indicate a timeline for responding to the situation, which will entail interviewing customers in question, other customers who may have observed, and library workers involved.

9. Resolution information or content as to how the situation was left with the customer should be communicated in a timely fashion. This content should also include any suggestions or corrective information regarding worker or volunteer techniques for handling future customer service situations.

Examples of Language Used to Communicate Customer Service Issues

Inappropriate Language	What's Wrong	Recommended Language
This customer complained about using the computers last night. He asked for the manager's name and number.	Too vague! No specific language, no information about what happened at the time, and no information about what library workers did to handle/resolve the issue at the time.	At 7:00 p.m. last night—while the librarian was handling the program in the meeting room—a customer, after waiting at reference for a few minutes, came to circulation. He appeared to be very angry and stated that he "had been waiting for 30 minutes at the reference desk and no one was there and no signs were posted." He indicated he was having "trouble finding books on the computer" and needed help. I apologized for the lack of service and the wait and gave him the "cheat sheet" for finding books. I asked him to wait while I went to check on where the librarian might be, but he said he couldn't wait any longer and "what poor service this was" and that he "wanted to complain to management and to the city." I took his name and number and gave him a card of the librarian on duty and the manager. I asked him to submit a customer response form and told him he would receive a call back within the next business day.
A customer came in acting like an idiot. She cursed at me and said I was stupid and said I didn't know how to do my job and wanted to complain about me. I didn't do anything wrong!!!!	Language is not neutral; name calling is unnecessary; there is only vague information; and defensive behavior is not helpful or informative.	I helped a customer yesterday morning. She came in and complained about a number of things in a loud voice (several workers observed this) and asked me to help her with a computer. I could not leave the circ desk and told her I could not leave but I could get someone to help her. She stated, "I must be stupid and lazy if I can't help her." I was too surprised and flustered to suggest the customer complaint form! She did take the manager's business card on the desk and left. I don't know if she will be back or complaining but I wanted to report it.

SAMPLE INCIDENT REPORT FORM

Branch: _____

Date and time of incident: _____

Location where incident occurred: _____

Describe the incident (that is, what occurred) as reported by:

☐ Library worker   ☐ Witness   ☐ Patron involved

_____

_____

_____

_____

_____

_____

Names and addresses of persons injured and/or description of property damaged:

_____

_____

Witnesses (include addresses): _____

_____

Action taken (first aid, called police, etc.): _____

_____

Comments: _____

_____

_____

_____

_____

Please check one: Customer ___ Accident ___ Assault ___ Illness ___ Other ___

Signed: _____ Job title: _____

Date: _____ Phone: _____

Retain copy in the branch and forward copies to your supervisor and the administrative office.

Resource H: Works Consulted

The following bibliography contains works consulted in the preparation of this book that were not either listed with annotations or footnoted in the text.

Monographs

Anderson, Kristin. *Great Customer Service on the Telephone.* New York: AMACOM (American Management Association), 1992.

Anderson, Kristin and Ron Zemke. *Coaching Knock Your Socks Off Service.* New York: AMACOM (American Management Association), 1991. 148 p.

Anderson, Kristin and Ron Zemke. *Delivering Knock Your Socks Off Service.* New York: AMACOM (American Management Association), 1991.

Armistead, Colin G. *Outstanding Customer Service: Implementing the Best Ideas from Around the World.* Irwin Professional Publishing., 1993.

Bacal, Robert. *Perfect Phrases for Customer Service: Hundreds of Tools, Techniques, and Scripts for Handling Any Situation.* New York: McGraw-Hill, 2005. 222 p.

Be Our Guest: Perfecting the Art of Customer Service. New York: Disney Institute, 2003. 206 p.

Bell, Chip, and Ron Zemke. *Managing Knock Your Socks Off Service.* New York: AMACOM (American Management Association), 1992.

Customers, Process Improvement, and Financial Results. Milwaukee: ASQ Quality Press, 2001. 340 p.

Customer Service and Sales Skills Standards. Sales and Service Voluntary Partnership, Inc., 2002.

Deep, Samuel D. *What to Say to Get What You Want: Strong Words for 44 Challenging Types of Bosses, Employees, Coworkers, and Customers.* Addison-Wesley, 1992.

Gee, Jeff and Val Gee. *Super Service: Seven Keys to Delivering Great Customer Service Even When You Don't Feel Like It, Even When They Don't Deserve It.* New York: McGraw-Hill, 1999.

Ginott, Haim G. *Between Parent and Child: The Bestselling Classic that Revolutionized Parent-Child Communication.* New York: Three Rivers Press, 2003.

Ginott, Haim G. *Between Parent and Teenager.* New York: Avon Books, 1988, 1972.

Ginott, Haim G. *Teacher and Child: A Book for Parents and Teachers.* New York: Avon Books, 1987. 251 p.

Hernon, Peter and Ellen Altman. *Assessing Service Quality: Satisfying the Expectations of Library Customers.* Chicago and London: American Library Association, 1998. 243 p.

Himmel, Edith, and William J. Wilson, with ReVision Committee of the Public Library Association. *Planning for Results: A Public Library Transformation Process.* Part 1: "How to Manual"; Part 2: "Guidebook." Chicago: American Library Association, 1998.

Lenz, Vicki. *The Saturn Difference: Creating Customer Loyalty in Your Company.* NY: Wiley, 1999. 274 p.

Jones, Patrick, and Joel Shoemaker. *Do It Right! Best Practices for Serving Young Adults in School and Public Libraries.* New York: Neal-Schuman, 2001. 182 p.

McClendon, Bruce W. *Customer Service in Local Government: Challenge for Planners and Managers*. Chicago, Ill." Planner's Press, 1992.

Melling, Maxine and Joyce Little. *Building a Successful Customer Service Culture: A Guide for Library and Information Managers*. New York: Neal-Schuman, 2002. 224 p.

Morgan, Rebecca. *Calming Upset Customers*. Crisp Publications, 1989.

Nauman, Earl and Steven H. Hoisington. *Customer Centered Six Sigma: Linking*

Nelson, Bob. *1001 Ways to Reward Employees*. New York: Workman, 1994. 275 p.

Nelson, Sandra. *The New Planning for Results: A Streamlined Approach*. Chicago: American Library Association, 2001. 315 p.

Rubin, Reah Joyce. *Defusing the Angry Patron: A How-to-Do-It Manual for Librarians*. New York: Neal-Schuman, 2000. 99 p.

Sanders, Betsy. *Fabled Service: Ordinary Acts, Extraordinary Outcomes*. San Francisco: Jossey-Bass, 1995. 127 p.

Seote, George. *Customer Service Programs in ARL Libraries*. Washington, D.C.; Association of Research Libraries, 1998.

Spector, Robert and Patrick McCarthy. *The Nordstrom Way to Customer Service Excellence: A Handbook for Implementing Great Service in Your Organization*. Hoboken, NJ: John Wiley and Sons, 2005. 270 p.

Wiersma, Fred. *Customer Service: Extraordinary Results at Southwest Airlines, Charles Schwab, Land's End, American Express, Staples, and USAA*. NY: Harper Business (Harper Collins), 1998. 234 p.

Zemke, Ron and Thomas K. Canaline. *Sustaining Knock Your Socks Off Service*. New York: AMACOM (American Management Association), 1993.

Periodicals

Armstrong, Larry. "Beyond, 'May I help you?'" *Business Week*. October 25, 1991: 101-103.

Berkeley, Susan, "Breaking Bad News to Customers: Soften the Blow," *Selling* (March 2004): 8.

Becker, Hal, "To Empower or Not to Empower: Don't Ask Such a Stupid Question," *Inside Business* 6, n. 1 (Jan 2004): 21.

Fossi, Frank, "Lesson Plan: Keeping Customers Satisfied-and Keeping Company Profits Healthy-Often Depends on How Well Customer Service Reps Are Trained," *HRMagazine* 48, n. 2 (Feb 2003): 72.

Galvin, Tammy, "Teaching Telephone Tactics," *Training* 41, n. 5 (May 2004): 14.

Hogan, Joyce and Robert Hogan. "How to Train and Hire Service-Oriented People." *Supervisory Management*. September 1989: 35-38.

Lawrence, S. "Distinctive Customer Service Traits." *Personnel Journal*. September 1990: 17.

Sanford, Kathleen D. "The Customer Isn't Always Right." *Supervisory Management*. October 1989: 29-32.

Snow, Dennis, "How to Create a Culture of Customer Service-A Checklist," *Patient Care Management* 19, n. 2 (Feb 2003): 7.

Sunoo, Brenda Park, "Results-Oriented Customer Service Training," *Workforce* 80, n. 5 (May 2001): 84.

Todaro, Julie. " Make 'em Smile." *School Library Journal.* January, 1995: 24-29.

"Training Strategies: Two Key Factors Are Essential in Customer Service Training," *Managing Training & Development* (Jan 2002): 1.

"The 3 Most Important Strategies to Include in Customer Service Training," *Managing Training and Development* (Sept 2002): 2.

Websites

Association of Library Services to Children. "Competencies for Librarians Serving Children in Public Libraries, Revised Edition." [Online]. Available: www.ala.org/ala/alsc/alscresources/forlibrarians/professionaldev/competencies.htm Last updated: April 27, 1999.

Bertland, Linda. Resources for School Librarians. "School Library Standards and Evaluation, Part 3." [Online]. Available: www.sldirectory.com/libsf/resf/statistics.html [2006, January 8].

Business Link. Achieving Best Practice in Your Business. [Online]. Available: www.businesslink.gov.uk/ 2006, January 9]

McNamara, Carter. "Quality Management." Free Management Library. [Online]. Available: www.managementhelp.org/quality/quality.htm 10 Oct. 2005.

National Institute of Standards and Technology. Baldrige National Quality Program. [Online]. Available: baldrige.nist.gov/ Last updated:1/4/2006.

Think & Do. Think & Do: Cultivating Customer Relationships. [Online]. Available: www.thinkanddo.us.

U.S. National Institutes of Health. National Library of Medicine. Fact Sheet: Reference and Web Services, "Customer Service Policy." [Online]. Available: www.nlm.nih.gov/pubs/factsheets/ref_serv.html Last updated: 8/30/2005.

Index

About the Authors

Julie Beth Todaro, Ph.D. has been a library manager and consultant for over 30 years. She specializes in the management of all types of libraries in the areas of twenty-first-century customer services, human resources issues, strategic planning, organizational design and effectiveness, community partnerships, and information literacy. Her professional career includes academic library manager for 22 years (community college) library school educator (public library specialist and management of nonprofits), and public librarian (children's and young adult). Julie also has her all-level school library certification. She has been closely involved with a variety of initiatives for all types of libraries, including serving as the chair of a committee to develop statewide standards for school libraries; the chair of a committee to implement a statewide public library study; and the cochair of the Information Literacy Community Partnerships initiative for the ACRL's Institute for Information Literacy. Julie was named a 2005 "Profiles in Power" winner by the *Austin Business Journal* in 2005 and is past president of the Texas Library Association from 2000 to 2001. The Texas Library Association has honored her as the Librarian of the Year in 1996, and she received the YWCA Austin Educator of the Year Award in 1999. She was chosen in 2006 as one of the seven providers for the PLA's Certified Public Library Administrator Program with her workshop "Staffing Issues for the 21st Century." Julie holds a master's degree in library and information science from The University of Texas at Austin and a doctorate in library services from Columbia University.

Mark Smith is the Vice President for Public Library Operations/West for Library Systems and Services, in which capacity he manages the Riverside County Library System, a 29-library system in Southern California. Mark has been a library manager and administrator for over 20 years. Before moving to California in 1999, he served as the Director of Communications for the Texas Library Association and as the Library Systems Administrator for the Texas State Library and Archives Commission. He was the director of the Plainsboro and Hillsdale Public Libraries in New Jersey between 1986 and 1991. Mark is the author of numerous books and articles, including the *Internet Policy Handbook for Libraries*

(Neal-Schuman, 1999) and *Collecting and Using Public Library Statistics* (Neal-Schuman, 1996), and the editor of *Managing the Internet Controversy* (Neal-Schuman, 2001). He has served as the chair of the Legislative Committees of the Public Library Association and the California Library Association and was honored as the California Library Association Member of the Year in 2003. Mark holds a master's degree in library and information science from the University of Texas at Austin.